Dear Beatrice,

This is my favourite play & the lead character is a very funny, proud & strong woman called Beatrice - just like you. I hope you enjoy it when you are older.

Happy 1st birthday, little one.

with love from

Sarah & Bobby

x x x

Much Ado About Nothing: A Comedy

William Shakespeare, William W. Lloyd

BIBLIOLIFE

PRINCEPS EDITION.

MUCH ADO ABOUT NOTHING:

A COMEDY

BY

WILLIAM SHAKESPEARE.

NOW FIRST PUBLISHED IN FULLY- RECOVERED

METRICAL FORM

AND WITH A

PREFATORY ESSAY

BY

WILLIAM WATKISS LLOYD.

London:

FREDERIC NORGATE,

KING STREET, COVENT GARDEN.

1884.

PREFATORY ESSAY.

THE distinctive and original feature of the projected and indeed prepared, edition of Shakespeare, of which this play is a specimen, is the recovery and exhibition of the proper character of the speeches hitherto uniformly printed for pure prose, as being in truth metrical,—composed by the poet in a very definite form of blank verse.

This metrical character, as peculiar as it is decided, is demonstrable not merely in particular cases of these speeches, but universally; by the recognition of it, a new light is thrown on the resources of English versification, and for the first time we attain to a full sense of the harmonious and expressive emphasis which Shakespeare imparted to his language, by a command of these resources, as infallible as it seems spontaneous.

It is certain that no one play of Shakespeare was printed with the benefit of the author's supervision; it remains impossible, therefore, to tell in what form he would have cast the speeches in question, had he survived to publish his own works. It does not appear that Ben Jonson, or any other of the leading contemporary dramatists, recognised any intermediate form of blank verse, between the normal line of ten or eleven syllables of five accented feet,—the so-called heroic verse,— and pure and simple prose, more or less familiar and colloquial. Nay, it may be admitted as even possible, that had Shakespeare himself printed " Much Ado about Nothing," he might only have given the form of verse to speeches which accommodate themselves to the familiar heroic line. But, nevertheless, it would remain consistent and conceivable, in regard to the rest of his work, that while writing a continuous text, he still, with music in his soul, instinctively adopted and adhered to specific rhythmical types as prompted by the spirit of particular characters and scenes; that a speech so written should be found on examination to fall into lines systematically divisible, would be no more strange than that a melody hastily noted by a composer should be susceptible of duly inserted bars.

The verdict of the ear is in both cases decided and decisive; under the suggestion, and then under the guidance of an ear for systematic metre, a principle becomes apparent that proves susceptible of the very largest application. It is found that the poet, in these speeches of reputed prose, retained for the most part the principle of giving five accented feet to a verse, as in his distinctly heroic verse; but he did so with a difference: he renounced the limitation of lines to ten or at most twelve syllables, and boldly broke into systems of lines in which the five accents were connected with feet consisting of three, four, or even more syllables, as frequently as of two.

It must be said that this revelation of a momentous secret of Shakespeare's dramatic skill and power, is not without confirmation, by no means insignificant, in the original printed texts. Not a few speeches, which the editors with one consent have reduced to plain prose, appear in the quartos and the folio in form of metre to which they have true claim if only duly distributed. But accurate distribution lamentably fails; and, from the ruling pedantic notions respecting versification, this semblance of metre has been misconstrued; it has been on all hands too easily ascribed to the carelessness and confusion which in other cases miserably disarranged lines that should take order of themselves as blank verse of the strictest type.

All metre depends, at last, upon equality of successive, well-marked divisions of time; but the equality of the intervals between marking accents is manifestly open to be maintained by equable, or accommodated by variable, rapidity of pronunciation; so it is, that associated bars in music are occupied by variable numbers of notes, and indeed of syllables to be sung to them, making up equivalent time. This variability, like any other, becomes an element and instrument of expression.

Milton was a master of the harmonies of versification, but the stateliness of his theme did not encourage laxity; even so we have such exceptional lines as these:—

> Wallowing, unwieldy, enormous in their gait—
> Of sorrow unfeigned and humiliation meek—

The licence admitted here is scarcely less than that of such lines as—

> How many gentlemen have you lost in this action?—
> Better bettered expectation than you must expect—

associated with a line as regular as—

> But few of any sort and none of name.

The variety in rapidity and the rhythmical contrasts which the dramatic poet thus gained command of, are of extra-ordinary compass and value; scenes once read as prose, not improved by shocks of unexpectedly stumbling into occasional rhythm, are found, when their metrical regulation is made manifest, to flow on with a full and unchecked tide of admirable music, from beginning to end.

The accurate division of the lines of any poetical text —of a dramatic text especially—is of great importance for guidance to inflection of voice and emphasis, whether in reading or declamation. It is characteristic of English blank verse, that proper rhetorical emphasis most frequently reinforces the accent of the first foot of the verse, with the natural result of involving the reduction in force of those which ensue:

> To bé or not to be,—that is the question;
> Whéther 'tis better that the body suffer, &c.—

This subordination prepares for the contrasted force at the beginning of the next line; the secondary accents may be of different values among themselves while relatively they accommodate the recurrence of stronger emphasis in its expected place. If this place is not made manifest to the eye of the reader, the rhythmical key is missing, and effort, unwarned, is liable to be exhausted prematurely upon words or phrases which, in their particular relation, have inferior claims. It is from the importance of giving opportunity for the first emphatic accent of an ensuing line, that a certain delicate intimation of a pause or suspension is required at the end of the line antecedent,— a pause very often beyond what might be challenged by strict rules of grammatical dependence. The due management of this often evanescent pause is the rarest refinement in the delivery of blank verse, and the acquisition of it demands the aid of an accurate distribution of text. And if such aid is necessary in the case of the strictly regulated heroic verse, it is still more indispensable

in a series of verses of which the very principle is eman-
cipation from restriction in favour of interchanges of tone
that shall have all the calculated value of piquant surprise.

In the adoption—the invention—of his freer forms of
versification, Shakespeare was following the precedent of
the poets of antiquity, as unconsciously to himself, no doubt,
as unsuspectedly even by others who had familiar know-
ledge both of Greek and Latin literature. The versification
of the epic poets, Homer and Virgil, moves on under far
stricter laws than even Milton, also an epic poet, was
required or chose to confine himself to. Their syllables are
either long or short—are wholes or halves—which cannot
interchange places and values; the utmost that can be
said is, that some of their long syllables are effectively
longer, and some short are shorter than others, and that
varied speed of pronunciation is easily responsible for
controlling and compensating these minor differences. A
greater variety of feet and values of syllables was admitted
in the senarian—the verse of six accented feet, of the
tragic poets, which answers in dialogue to Shakespeare's
ten-syllable verse. But still this form of verse was
subject, in their hands, to certain limitations which were
very positive,—limitations of which some of the most
positive were renounced without scruple, when it was
adopted by the comic poets, who at last seem to have
been quite content so long as versification at all remained
recognisable. Still, ancient comedy held pertinaciously to
versification; laxly or licentiously as it was there dealt with,
it was susceptible all the more of management with playful
and inventive versatility. If the question was argued in
antiquity, whether comedies were rightly called poems, the
dispute turned at last, not on the value of their metrical
forms, but on the propriety of dignifying the themes which
they descended to—conversation at best, and at lowest,
vulgar banter—with so superb a title. In the meantime, the
noble lyric poets, Pindar especially, had in an entirely
opposite direction released themselves from any obligation
to regard the number of syllables in associated metrical
feet, in any other relation than would be recognised by a
musician.

Hence it was that Cicero could say that the verses of the
finest Greek lyric poets were liable to become, but for
the assistance of music, apparently destitute of metrical

character at all; the succession of syllables, in fact, required, to his appreciation, to be grouped by subsidiary accentuation, vocal or instrumental, if they were not to resolve themselves into prose; his ear required the same help—it may seem to us as we may now read Pindar rather strange that it should be so—that is here proffered —not too soon—to the eye, for the vindication of Shakespeare's comic metre.

In a certain number of peculiar cases, Shakespeare employs with the greatest effect an equable line of six instead of five of his freer accented feet, through a speech or even an entire scene. Otherwise what might be mistaken for occasional lines of six accents are often divisible into pairs of triplet accents, and are better so exhibited typographically. Another important variation which has not entirely escaped attention, so far as concerns ten-syllable lines, is the case of what may be called interlaced lines. Incomplete lines, usually half-lines, occur, which admit of being read as completions of portions of the lines that precede, or, in other cases, that follow them; it is again of importance to due recognition of the metre, that any such incomplete line should be duly distinguished as it is the commencement or the end of an interlacement. Unless this difference is exhibited, an accent of false strength will be placed precisely where it damages a cadence.

Metrical licence was carried to its extreme by the authors of the later Greek comedy, and Cicero (Orator LII) can say of them that their senarians had frequently such resemblance to common discourse, and were so negligently indicated, that, as he found with the verses of the lyric poets, it was often scarcely possible to recognise in them any metrical character. It is not quite clear whether he appreciated all the same the appropriateness of such versification to the freedom of comedy, and the apt skill displayed in its management. Quintilian (X, I, 918) at least has no sympathy for the varied schemes of verse which Terence plays with, and he never writes so much like a scholastic pedant as when he expresses a wish that an author so elegant had confined himself to the single senarian form of verse.

To compensate in some degree for the loss of the new Greek comedians, we have in Terence and Plautus examples of how the ancients married comic motives and dialogue

representative of common life, with varied and appropriate
metrical forms of true artistic finish.   The following obser-
vations of Erasmus on the versification of Terentian comedy,
have been fully borne out by the study of more recent
scholars, with Bentley at their head, and are applicable in
ultimate result to what we shall see of the practice of
Shakespeare.   Shakespeare assuredly was under no obligation to any ancient for the hint; the common sympathies of
poetic genius are sufficient to account for the coincidence.
Nature is not so economical of her suggestiveness as to limit
herself to a single intimation of a principle, leaving the world
thereafter to take its precarious chance of making the best
of it, in case it survives, by processes of evolution.

"The Latin writers of comedy," says Erasmus, "allowed
themselves much liberty in versification, and none more
than Terence; he indeed so extensively that some have
even concluded that he observed no rules of verse whatever.
The mistake made by these is manifest.   There were
others again who did not deny that he attended to rules of
metre, but concluded that from his immoderate licence it
was not worth the while of the learned to plague themselves
with scanning the verses, as it would be a matter of great
labour with very little profit at last.   For my own part, I
disagree with both; for as no proof is really required that
the comedies of Terence are in verse, so those who thought
his metrical system might be neglected have repeatedly
corrupted the poet's language by substituting one word for
another (an incident too frequent with copyists of prose
authors) by additions, omissions, or inversions of the order
of words.   Even the learned have somewhat sinned in the
same way, who in default of study have, in the process of
distinguishing and scanning classes of verses, interpolated
words to fill up a supposed gap or cut away a seeming
redundancy.   It appears, however, to have been distinctly
intentional on the part of Terence, to make the nearest
approach possible, by verse in disguised form (*dissimulato
carmine*), to the language of prose,—the same purpose that
Horace seems to have had in view in his Satires and
Epistles."

The metrical systems of both Terence and Plautus have
been made the subject of profound study since the time of
Erasmus; and we may now have the advantage of editions
in which the metrical accents are marked, and facility is

given for appreciating the skill with which the expression
of humour, sentiment, or passion, is heightened by appropriate rhythm, and the charm of harmonious versification is
fully restored. " Above all," says a recent editor of Plautus,
" the rhythmical accents have been inserted throughout
this edition, following the precedent of Bentley's Terence,
inasmuch as only in virtue of such aid can Plautus be read
as he ought to be, not as a prose author, but rhythmically
as a true poet."

In the case of Shakespeare there is no need to mark
accents; but the necessity is the more absolute for his
metrically constructed lines to be so divided as to give
the assistance which is indispensable, if he is to be read
with comfort and confidence, and full enjoyment of his
marvellous rhythmical harmonies and constantly varying
characteristic tone and style,—if he too is to be read, not as
a prose author, but as a poet chiefly, as a poet always.

When we compare the more free verses of Plautus with
the severely regulated measures of the hexameter and the
senarian, we find that they have great analogy to the form
of verse which Shakespeare employed in the speeches which
have been, as uniformly as falsely and unfortunately, printed
as prose. In these it will be found that sequences of feet
are marked off by accents which so strongly reinforce the
natural accents of the emphatic words or phrases, as to
perfectly subordinate those which carry no especial emphasis. In consequence, although in the great majority of
cases the rule of five feet in a line is still observed, the
frequency of trisyllabic feet is much increased; feet containing even more syllables are not unusual, and all forms
of redundancy of syllables at the end or commencement of
a verse are more freely admitted.

To versification in this form, still more than to ordinary
blank verse of high character, does the rule apply that the
places of reinforced emphatic accent are decided by no
fixed rule; they are discoverable only by intelligent
reading or expressive declamation. The true distribution
and regulation of the lines, as certified by revelation of
poetic expression in full force, is even so in many cases
not to be determined until after many trials and comparisons. A metrical speech printed as prose—a speech of
such metrical character as is in question—is "a tangled
chain, nothing impaired, but all disordered." The process

of disentanglement is often the more difficult from the very elaborateness and refinement of the workmanship of the chain; but when it is once effected, these very qualities are testimony to the success. From what has been said of the interlacements of verse usual with Shakespeare, it will be quite understood that a prose printed speech often includes what seems to be an indisputable independent verse, but which, nevertheless, is of right to be distributed between two successive verses. If such a false end of a clue be retained too obstinately, all that follows and all that precedes will be thrown out of metrical gear. The same will be the case if one of the loose half-lines of which examples are abundant should be forcibly worked in as portion of an independent and complete line. On the other hand, guidance most welcome and decisive is often ministered by the occurrence of successive lines that reveal themselves as certainly self-limited.

There are thus many difficulties and false lights that mislead and frustrate first attempts; is it possible that these have disheartened some explorers prematurely and caused them to renounce the inquiry, and even keep silence as to ever having entertained a suspicion of its value? Some explanation seems certainly required for the world of criticism having remained blind so long to a fact which is glaring as soon as it is pointed out.

Finally to clench the entire argument, for those by whom argument may be challenged to vindicate the decision of simple refined instinct of rhythm and cadence, let due weight be given to this observation:—

No licences of versification will be found to be presumed on for the reduction of the complete dramatic text to metrical form, for which authoritative precedents are not citable from speeches which have always been accepted and printed as verse. In some of these speeches the exceptionally constituted lines are rare enough or missing; in others they are even numerous and in close succession. But whether few or many, interposed and interlinked as they are, they have never roused suspicion of being other than truly metrical. Truly metrical, therefore, such lines must be no less when, as in the speeches now for the first time reconstituted, they as a rule preponderate above associated lines of the common normal type, and even exclude such altogether.

Let the dialogue between Iago and Roderigo at the opening of "Othello" serve to exemplify both the variable frequency and the variety in themselves, of such interpolated and interwoven abnormal lines, which in virtue of position have passed muster without question or protest.

The same speeches supply opportunities, at the commencement of the extract, for indicating the metrical dependence of loose half-lines by reformed typographical ordination.

Enter RODERIGO *and* IAGO.

Rod. Tush ! Never tell me ; I take it much unkindly
That thou, Iago, who hast had my purse
As if the strings were thine, shouldst know of this.
 Iago. 'Sblood, but you will not hear me :—
       If ever I did dream of such a matter,
Abhor me.
  Rod. Thou told'st me thou didst hold him in thy hate.
  Iago.   Despise me
If I do not. Three great ones of the city,
In personal suit to make me his lieutenant,
Off-capped to him :—and, by the faith of man,
I know my price, I am worth no worse a place :
But he, as loving his own pride and purposes,
Evades them, with a bombast circumstance
Horribly stuffed with epithets of war ;
        And, in conclusion,
Nonsuits my mediators ; for, "Certes," says he,
"I have already chose my officer." And what
Was he ? Forsooth, a great arithmetician,
One Michael Cassio, a Florentine,
A fellow almost damned in a fair wife ;
That never set a squadron in the field,
Nor the division of a battle knows
More than a spinster ; unless the bookish theoric,
Wherein the toged consuls can propose
As masterly as he : mere prattle, without practice,
Is all his soldiership. But he, sir, had the election :
And I,—of whom his eyes had seen the proof
At Rhodes, at Cyprus, and on other grounds,
Christian and heathen,—must be be-lee'd and calmed
By debitor-and-creditor, this counter-caster ;
He, in good time, must his lieutenant be,
And I—God bless the mark !—his Moorship's ancient.
 Rod. By heaven, I rather would have been his hangman.
 Iago. Why, there's no remedy ; 'tis the curse of service,
Preferment goes by letter and affection,
And not by old gradation, where each second
Stood heir to the first. Now, sir, be judge yourself,
Whether I, in any just term, am affined
To love the Moor.

Rod.   I would not follow him then,
Iago.   O, sir, content you ;
I follow him to serve my turn upon him :
We cannot all be masters, nor all masters
Cannot be truly followed.   You shall mark
Many a duteous and knee-crooking knave,
That, doting on his own obsequious bondage,
Wears out his time, much like his master's ass,
For nought but provender ; and when he's old, cashiered :
Whip me such honest knaves.   Others there are,
Who, trimmed in forms and visages of duty,
Keep yet their hearts attending on themselves ;
And, throwing but shows of service on their lords,
Do well thrive by them, and, when they have lined their coats
Do themselves homage : these fellows have some soul :
And such a one do I profess myself.   For, sir,
It is as sure as you are Roderigo,
Were I the Moor, I would not be Iago :
In following him, I follow but myself ;
Heaven is my judge, not I for love and duty,
But seeming so, for my peculiar end.

This extract taken alone is sufficient to show how the numbers and the places of the trisyllabic and still more polysyllabic feet which are admitted by the poet, are subject to interchanges and permutations that would almost defy tabulation ; there proves in consequence to be as much scope for characteristic variation in the internal construction of these more loosely regulated lines, as in the groups or alternations by which they diversify sequences of forms more normally constituted.

What wonder that Shakespeare, after shaking himself clear of the last trammels of tradition in versification, appears exultant in the exercise of his self-achieved freedom ; but at the same time that he is exhaustless in his invention of opportunities for variation of rhythmical harmony, he ever displays full command over himself in controlling its application,—in evolving its resources under subjection ever to a dominant ideal born of the occasion.

"Shakespeare, it has been well said, most assuredly wrote without any reference to rule ; he trusted to his ear, and produced the finest dramatic verse in the world. Milton, also, beyond all competition the greatest writer of epic verse that we can boast, learned as he was both in metres and music, and with finest apprehension of harmony, evidently composed without rule, and trusted to his ear alone for those exquisite cadences with which, from his Lycidas to his Paradise Regained, his poems abound" (*Quarterly Review*, 1825, p. 34). It is added: "To deduce authoritatively rules from poems that have been written without rule, is plainly to derive an argument in favour of bondage from the most splendid proofs of the benefits of freedom." But to deduce rules which are to be insisted on as generally authoritative is one thing; to elicit the rules which a poet allowed to govern him as contrasted with those which he disregarded is another; it is to set forth how the privileges of freedom are exercised by the highest poetic genius under spontaneously yielded allegiance to recondite law.

PERSONS REPRESENTED.

DON PEDRO, *Prince of* ARRAGON.

DON JOHN, *his bastard Brother.*

COUNT CLAUDIO, *a young Lord of* FLORENCE.

SIGNIOR BENEDICK, *a young Lord of* PADUA.

LEONATO, *Governor of* MESSINA.

ANTONIO, *his elder Brother.*

BALTHAZAR, *Attendant on* DON PEDRO.

BORACHIO
CONRADE } *followers of* DON JOHN.

DOGBERRY, *Head Constable.*

VERJUICE, *his Partner.*

GEORGE SEACOAL, *Constable of the Watch.*

FRANCIS SEACOAL, *the Sexton.*

FRIAR FRANCIS.

MESSENGER *from* DON PEDRO.

HERO, *daughter to* LEONATO.

BEATRICE, *niece and ward to* LEONATO.

MARGARET
URSULA } *gentlewomen attending on* HERO.

A boy, Messenger, Watchmen, and Attendants.

SCENE—MESSINA.

MUCH ADO ABOUT NOTHING.

ACT I.

SCENE I.—*A Garden;* LEONATO'S *House behind.*

Enter LEONATO, HERO, BEATRICE, *and others, with a*
MESSENGER.

Leonato.

LEARN from this letter that Don Pedro of
Arragon
Comes this night to Messina.

  Mess.   He is very near by this:
He was not three leagues off when I left him.

 Leon. How many gentlemen have you lost in this action?

 Mess. But few of any sort, and none of name.

 Leon. A victory is twice itself, when the achiever
Brings home full numbers. I find here that Don Pedro
Hath bestowed much honour on a young Florentine
Called Claudio.

  Mess.   Much deserved on his part, and equally
Remembered by Don Pedro: he hath borne himself
Beyond the promise of his age; doing in the figure
Of a lamb the feats of a lion: he hath, indeed,
Better bettered expectation than you must expect
Of me to tell you how.

 Leon.   He hath an uncle
Here in Messina will be very much glad of it.

 Mess. I have already delivered him letters, and there
Appears much joy in him; even so much, that joy
Could not show itself modest enough without
A badge of bitterness.

Leon.   Did he break out into tears?

Mess. In great measure.

Leon.   A kind overflow of kindness:
There are no faces truer than those that are so washed.
How much better it is to weep at joy than to
Joy at weeping!

Beat.   I pray you, is Signior Montanto
Returned from the wars, or no?

Mess. I know none of that name, lady:
There was none such in the army of any sort.

Leon. What is he that you ask for, niece?

Hero.   My cousin
Means Signior Benedick of Padua.

Mess. O, he is returned; and as pleasant as ever he was.

Beat. He set up his bills here in Messina,
And challenged Cupid at the flight; and my uncle's fool,
Reading the challenge, subscribed for Cupid, and challenged
Him at the bird bolt.   I pray you, how many hath he killed
And eaten in these wars?   But how many hath he killed?
For, indeed, I promised to eat all of his killing.

Leon. Faith, niece, you tax Signior Benedick too much;
But he'll be meet with you, I doubt it not.

Mess. He hath done good service, lady, in these wars.

Beat. You had musty victual, and he hath holp to eat it:
He is a very valiant trencher-man; he hath
An excellent stomach.

Mess.   And a good soldier too, lady.

Beat. And a good soldier to a lady;—but what is he
To a lord?

Mess.   A lord to a lord, a man to a man;
Stuffed with all honourable virtues.

Beat.   It is so, indeed;
He is no less than a stuffed man: but for the stuffing,—
Well, we are all mortal.

Leon.   You must not, sir, mistake my niece:
There is a kind of merry war betwixt

Signior Benedick and her; they never meet
But there is a skirmish of wit between them.

Beat.   Alas, he gets
Nothing by that!   In our last conflict, four
Of his five wits went halting off, and now
Is the whole man governed with one; so that if he have
    wit enough
To keep himself warm, let him bear it for a difference
Between himself and his horse; for it is all the wealth
That he hath left, to be known a reasonable creature.—
Who is his companion now?   He hath every month
A new sworn brother.

Mess.   Is it possible?

Beat. Very easily possible: he wears his faith but as
The fashion of his hat; it ever changes
With the next block.

Mess.   I see, lady, the gentleman
Is not in your books.

Beat.   No; an he were,
I would burn my study.   But, I pray you, who is
His companion?   Is there no young squarer now, that
Will make a voyage with him to the devil?

Mess. He is most in the company of the right noble
    Claudio.

Beat. O Lord! he will hang upon him like a disease:
He is sooner caught than the pestilence, and the taker
Runs presently mad.   God help the noble Claudio!
If he have caught the Benedick, it will cost him
    A thousand pound ere he be cured.

Mess. I will hold friends with you, lady.

Beat.   Do, good friend.

Leon. You will never run mad, niece.

Beat.   No, not till a hot
January.

Mess.   Don Pedro is approached.

Enter DON PEDRO, DON JOHN, CLAUDIO, BENEDICK,
BALTHAZAR, *and others.*

D. Pedro. Good Signior Leonato, are you come
To meet your trouble? the fashion of the world is
To avoid cost, and you encounter it.

Leon. Never came trouble to my house in the likeness
Of your grace: for trouble being gone,
Comfort should remain; but when you depart from me,
Sorrow abides, and happiness takes his leave.

D. Pedro. You embrace your charge too willingly.—I
    think
This is your daughter.

Leon.   Her mother hath many times
Told me so.

Bene.   Were you in doubt, sir, that you asked her?

Leon. Signior Benedick, no; for then were you a child.

D Pedro. You have it full, Benedick; we may guess by
    this,
What you are, being a man.—Truly, the lady
Fathers herself. Be happy, lady; for you are like
An honourable father.

Bene.   If Signior Leonato be her father,
She would not have his head on her shoulders for all
Messina, as like him as she is.

Beat.   I wonder
That you will still be talking, Signior Benedick:
Nobody marks you.

Bene.   What, my dear lady Disdain!
Are you yet living?

Beat.   Is it possible Disdain
Should die, while she hath such meet food to feed it,
As Signior Benedick? Courtesy itself must
Convert to disdain, if you come in her presence.

Bene. Then is courtesy a turn-coat.—But it is certain
I am loved of all ladies, only you excepted:

And I would I could find in my heart that I had not
A hard heart; for, truly, I love none.

 Beat.   A dear
Happiness to women: they would else have been troubled
With a pernicious suitor. I thank God and
My cold blood, I am of your humour for that:
I had rather hear my dog bark at a crow,
Than a man swear he loves me.

 Bene.   God keep your ladyship
Still in that mind! so some gentleman or other
Shall 'scape a predestinate scratched face.

 Beat.   Scratching could not
Make it worse, an 'twere such a face as yours were.

 Bene. Well, you are a rare parrot-teacher.

 Beat.   A bird of my tongue
Is better than a beast of yours.

 Bene.   I would my horse
Had the speed of your tongue, and so good a continuer.
But keep your way, o' God's name; I have done.

 Beat. You always end with a jade's trick: I know you
Of old.

 D. Pedro.   That is the sum of all, Leonato.
Signior Claudio and Signior Benedick,—my dear friend
Leonato hath invited you all. I tell him we shall
Stay here at the least a month; and he heartily prays
Some occasion may detain us longer: I dare swear
He is no hypocrite, but prays from his heart.

 Leon. If you swear, my lord, you shall not be forsworn.—
Let me bid you welcome, my lord: being reconciled
To the prince your brother, I owe you all duty.

 D. John.   I thank you;
I am not of many words, but I thank you.

 Leon. Please it your grace lead on?

 D. Pedro.   Your hand, Leonato;
We will go together.

    [*Exeunt all but* Benedick *and* Claudio.

Claud.   Benedick, didst thou note the daughter
Of Signior Leonato?

Bene.   I noted her not; but I looked on her.

Claud. Is she not a modest young lady?

Bene.   Do you question me, as
An honest man should do, for his simple true judgment;
Or would you have me speak after my custom,
As being a professed tyrant to their sex?

Claud.   No; I pray thee
Speak in sober judgment.

Bene.   Why, i' faith, methinks
She is too low for a high praise, too brown
For a fair praise, and too little for a great praise.
Only this commendation I can afford her,—
That were she other than she is, she were
Unhandsome; and being no other but as she is,
I do not like her.

Claud.   Thou thinkest I am in sport:
I pray thee tell me truly, how thou likest her.

Bene. Would you buy her that you inquire after her?

Claud. Can the world buy such a jewel?

Bene.   Yea, and a case
To put it into. But speak you this with a sad brow?
Or do you play the flouting Jack, to tell us
Cupid is a good hare-finder, and Vulcan a rare
Carpenter? Come, in what key shall a man take you,
To go in the song?

Claud.   In mine eye she is the sweetest
Lady that ever I looked on.

Bene.   I can see yet
Without spectacles, and I see no such matter:
There's her cousin an she were not possessed
With a fury, exceeds her as much in beauty as
The first of May doth the last of December. But
I hope you have no intent to turn husband,—have
    you?

Claud. I would scarce trust myself, though I had sworn
The contrary, if Hero would be my wife.

Bene. Is it come to this i' faith ?   Hath not the world
One man but he will wear his cap with suspicion ?
Shall I never see a bachelor of threescore again ?
Go to, i' faith ; an thou will needs thrust thy neck into a
        yoke,
Wear the print of it, and sigh away Sundays.
Look, Don Pedro is returned to seek you.

Re-enter Don Pedro.

D. Pedro. What secret hath held you here, that you
        followed not
To Leonato's ?

Bene.   I would your grace would constrain me
To tell.

D. Pedro.   I charge thee on thy allegiance.

Bene. You hear, Count Claudio : I can be as secret as
A dumb man, I would have you think so ; but on
My allegiance,—mark you this, on my allegiance.—
He is in love.   With who ?—now that is your grace's part,—
Mark, how short his answer is : With Hero, Leonato's
Short daughter.

Claud.   If this were so, so were it utterèd.

Bene. Like the old tale, my lord ; it is not so,
Nor 'twas not so ; but indeed, God forbid
It should be so.

Claud.   If my passion change not shortly,
God forbid it should be otherwise.

D. Pedro.   Amen, if you
Love her ; for the lady is well worthy.

Claud. You speak this to fetch me in, my lord.

D. Pedro.   By my troth,
I speak my thought.

Claud.   And, in faith, my lord, I spoke mine.

Bene. And, by my two faiths and troths, my lord, I spoke
  mine.

Claud. That I love her, I feel.

D. Pedro.   That she is worthy, I know.

Bene. That I neither feel how she should be loved, nor
  know
How she should be worthy, is the opinion that fire
Cannot melt out of me: I will die in it at the stake.

D. Pedro. Thou wast ever an obstinate heretic in the
  despite
Of beauty.

Claud.   And never could maintain his part,
But in the force of his will.

Bene.   That a woman conceived me,
I thank her; that she brought me up, I likewise
Give her most humble thanks: but that I will have a
  recheat
Winded in my forehead, or hang my bugle in an
Invisible baldric, all women shall pardon me.
Because I will not do them the wrong to mistrust
Any, I will do myself the right to trust none;
And the fine is (for the which I may go the finer)
I will live a bachelor.

D. Pedro.   I shall see thee, ere I die,
Look pale with love.

Bene.   With anger, with sickness, or with hunger,
My lord; not with love: prove that I ever lose
More blood with love than I will get again with drinking,
Pick out mine eyes with a ballad-maker's pen,
And hang me up at the door of a brothel-house
For the sign of blind Cupid.

D. Pedro.   Well, if ever thou dost fall
From this faith, thou wilt prove a notable argument.

Bene. If I do, hang me in a bottle like a cat, and shoot
  at me;

And he that hits me, let him be clapped on the shoulder,
    And called Adam.

D. Pedro.   Well, as time shall try:
"In time the savage bull doth bear the yoke."

Bene. The savage bull may; but if ever the sensible
Benedick bear it, pluck off the bull's horns, and
Set them in my forehead: and let me be vilely painted;
And in such great letters as they write, "Here is
Good horse to hire," let them signify under my sign,—
"Here you may see Benedick, the married man."

Claud. If this should ever happen, thou wouldst be
    horn-mad.

D. Pedro.   Nay,
If Cupid have not spent all his quiver in Venice,
Thou wilt quake for this shortly.

Bene.   I look for an earthquake
Too, then.

D. Pedro.   Well, you will temporise with the hours.
In the meantime, good Signior Benedick,
Repair to Leonato's: commend me to him, and tell him
I will not fail him at supper; for indeed
He hath made great preparation.

Bene.   I have almost matter
Enough in me for such an embassage, and so
I commit you—

Claud.   To the tuition of God:
From my house, (if I had it),—

D. Pedro.   The sixth of July:
Your loving friend, Benedick.

Bene.   Nay, mock not, mock not.
The body of your discourse is sometime guarded
With fragments, and the guards are but slightly
Basted on neither: ere you flout old ends any further,
Examine your consciences: and so I leave you.

                           [*Exit* BENEDICK.

Claud. My liege, your highness now may do me good.

D. Pedro. My love is thine to teach; teach it but how,
And thou shalt see how apt it is to learn
Any hard lesson that may do thee good.

Claud. Hath Leonato any son, my lord?

D. Pedro. No child but Hero; she's his only heir.
Dost thou affect her, Claudio?

Claud.   O, my lord,
When you went onward on this ended action,
I look'd upon her with a soldier's eye,
That lik'd, but had a rougher task in hand
Than to drive liking to the name of love:
But now I am return'd, and that war-thoughts
Have left their places vacant, in their rooms
Come thronging soft and delicate desires,
All prompting me how fair young Hero is,
Saying, I lik'd her ere I went to wars.—

D. Pedro. Thou wilt be like a lover presently,
And tire the hearer with a book of words.
If thou dost love fair Hero, cherish it;
And I will break with her, and with her father,
And thou shalt have her.   Was't not to this end,
That thou began'st to twist so fine a story?

Claud. How sweetly do you minister to love,
That know love's grief by his complexion!
But lest my liking might too sudden seem,
I would have salv'd it with a longer treatise.

D. Pedro. What need the bridge much broader than the
        flood?
The fairest grant is the necessity:
Look, what will serve, is fit: 'tis once, thou lov'st;
And I will fit thee with the remedy.
I know we shall have revelling to-night;
I will assume thy part in some disguise,
And tell fair Hero I am Claudio;
And in her bosom I'll unclasp my heart,

And take her hearing prisoner with the force
And strong encounter of my amorous tale:
Then, after, to her father will I break;
And, the conclusion is, she shall be thine.
In practice let us put it presently.   [*Exeunt.*

Scene II.—*A Room in* Leonato's *House.*

Enter severally Leonato *and* Antonio.

Leon. How now, brother? Where is my cousin, your
  son?
Hath he provided this music?
  Ant.   He is very
Busy about it.   But, brother, I can tell you
Strange news, that you yet dreamed not of.
  Leon.   Are they good?
  Ant. As the event stamps them; but they have a good
    cover,
They show well outward.   The prince and Count Claudio,
 Walking in a thick-pleached alley ofmy orchard,
Were thus much overheard by a man of mine:
The prince discovered to Claudio that he loved
My niece your daughter, and meant to acknowledge it
This night in a dance; and if he found her accordant,
He meant to take the present time by the top,
And instantly break with you of it.
  Leon.   Hath the fellow
Any wit that told you this?
  Ant.   A good sharp fellow:
I will send for him; and question him yourself.
  Leon.   No, no;
We will hold it but a dream, till it appears
Itself:—but I will acquaint my daughter withal,
That she may be better prepared for an answer,
              If peradventure, this be true.

    [*Several persons cross the stage.*]

Go you, and tell her of it.   Cousins, you know
What you have to do.—O, I cry you mercy, friend ;
Go you with me and I will use your skill ;—
Good cousin, have a care this busy time.

[*Exeunt.*

SCENE III.—*Another Room in* LEONATO'S *House.*

Enter DON JOHN *and* CONRADE.

Con. What the good-year, my lord! why are you out of
      measure
Sad ?

D. John. There is no measure in the occasion that breeds it ;
Therefore the sadness is without limit.

Con.   You should hear reason.

D. John. And when I have heard it, what blessing
      bringeth it ?

Con. If not a present remedy, yet a patient sufferance.

D. John. I wonder that thou, being (as thou say'st thou
      art)
Born under Saturn, goest about to apply
A moral medicine to a mortifying mischief.
I cannot hide what I am : I must be sad
When I have cause, and smile at no man's jests ;
Eat when I have stomach, and wait for no man's leisure ;
Sleep when I am drowsy, and tend on no man's business ;
Laugh when I am merry, and claw no man in his humour.

Con. Yea, but you must not make the full show of this,
Till you may do it without controlment.   You have
Until of late stood out against your brother,
And he hath ta'en you newly into his grace ;
Where it is impossible you should take true root,
But by the fair weather, that you make yourself : it is
Needful that you frame the season for your own harvest.

D. John. I had rather be a canker in a hedge than a rose
      in his grace ;

And it better fits my blood to be disdained of all,
Than to fashion a carriage to rob love from any.   In this,
Though I cannot be said to be a flattering honest man,
It must not be denied but I am a plain-dealing villain.
I am trusted with a muzzle and enfranchised with a clog;
Therefore I have decreed not to sing in my cage.   If I had
My mouth, I would bite; if I had my liberty, I would do
    my liking:
In the meantime let me be that I am, and seek not to
    alter me.
  Con. Can you make no use of your discontent?
  D. John.   I make all use of it,
For I use it only.—Who comes here?

Enter BORACHIO.

                        What news, Borachio?
  Bora. I came yonder from a great supper; the prince,
    your brother,
Is royally entertained by Leonato; and I can
Give you intelligence of an intended marriage.
  D. John. Will it serve for any model to build mischief
    on?
What is he for a fool that betroths himself
To unquietness?
  Bora.   Marry, it is your brother's right hand.
  D. John. Who? the most exquisite Claudio?
  Bora.   Even he.
  D. John. A proper squire! and who, and who? which
    way looks he?
  Bora. Marry, on Hero, the daughter and heir of Leonato.
  D. John. A very forward March chick! how came you
    to this?
  Bora. Being entertained for a perfumer, as I was smoking
A musty room, comes me the prince and Claudio,
Hand in hand, in sad conference; I whipt me behind
The arras; and there heard it agreed upon, that

The prince should woo Hero for himself, and having
Obtained her, give her to Count Claudio.

    D. John.   Come, come,
Let us thither; this may prove food to my displeasure.
That young start-up hath all the glory of my overthrow;
If I can cross him any way, I bless myself every way.
You are both sure, and will assist me?

    Con.   To the death, my lord.

    D. John. Let us to the great supper: their cheer is the
         greater that I
Am subdued. Would the cook were of my mind!—Shall
         we go prove
What's to be done?

    Bora.   We'll wait upon your lordship.

                            [*Exeunt.*

ACT II.

SCENE I.—*A Hall in* LEONATO'S *House.*

Enter LEONATO, ANTONIO, HERO, BEATRICE, *and others.*

Leonato.

AS not Count John here at supper?
 Ant.   I saw him not·
 Beat. How tartly that gentleman looks! I never
  can see him,
But I am heart-burned an hour after.
 Hero.   He is
Of a very melancholy disposition.
 Beat. He were an excellent man, that were made just
In the midway between him and Benedick:
The one is too like an image, and says nothing;
And the other too like my lady's eldest son,
Evermore tattling.
 Leon.   Then half Signior Benedick's tongue
In Count John's mouth, and half Count John's melancholy
In Signior Benedick's face,—
 Beat.   With a good leg,
And a good foot, uncle, and money enough in his purse,—
Such a man would win any woman in the world,—
If he could get her goodwill.
 Leon.   By my troth, niece,
Thou wilt never get thee a husband, if thou be so
Shrewd of thy tongue.
 Ant.   In faith, she is too curst.
 Beat. Too curst is more than curst: I shall lessen God's
  sending
That way; for it is said, "God sends a curst cow
Short horns;" but to a cow too curst he sends none.

Leon. So, by being too curst, God will send you no
    horns.

Beat. Just, if he send me no husband; for the which
    blessing

I am at him upon my knees every morning

And evening. Lord! I could not endure a husband

With a beard on his face: I had rather lie in the woollen.

Leon. You may light on a husband, that hath no beard.

Beat. What should I do with him? dress him in my
    apparel,

And make him my waiting gentlewoman?

He that hath a beard is more than a youth;

And he that hath no beard is less than a man:

And he that is more than a youth is not for me;

And he that is less than a man, I am not for him:

Therefore I will even take sixpence in earnest of the
    bearward,

And lead his apes into hell.

Leon.   Well, then, go you into hell?

Beat. No; but to the gate; and there will the devil
    meet me,

Like an old cuckold, with horns on his head, and say,

" Get you to heaven, Beatrice, get you to heaven;

Here's no place for you maids:" so deliver I up

My apes, and away to St. Peter for the heavens;

He shows me where the bachelors sit, and there

Live we as merry as the day is long.

Ant. [*To* HERO.]   Well, niece,

I trust you will be ruled by your father.

Beat.   Yes, faith;

It is my cousin's duty to make courtesy, and say,

" Father, as it please you:"—but yet, for all that, cousin,

Let him be a handsome fellow, or else make another

Courtesy, and say, " Father as it please me."

Leon.   Well, niece,

I hope to see you one day fitted with a husband.

Beat. Not till God make men of some other metal
Than earth.   Would it not grieve a woman to be
Overmastered with a piece of valiant dust? to make
An account of her life to a clod of wayward marl?
No, uncle, I'll none: Adam's sons are my brethren;
And, truly, I hold it a sin to match in my kindred.

    Leon. Daughter, remember what I told you: if the
        prince
Do solicit you in that kind, you know your answer.

    Beat. The fault will be in the music, cousin, if you be
        not
Wooed in good time: if the prince be too important,
Tell him there is a measure in everything, and so dance
        out
The answer.   For, hear me, Hero,—wooing, wedding,
And repenting, is as a Scotch jig, a measure, and a cinque-
        pace:
The first suit is hot and hasty, like a Scotch jig,
And full as fantastical; the wedding, mannerly-modest,
As a measure, full of state and ancientry; and then comes
Repentance, and with his bad legs, falls into the cinque-
        pace
Faster and faster, till he sink into his grave.

    Leon. Cousin, you apprehend passing shrewdly.

    Beat.   I have
A good eye, uncle; I can see a church by daylight.

    Leon. The revellers are entering; brother, make good
        room!

                      [*They all mask.*

Enter Don Pedro, Claudio, Benedick, Balthazar, Don
John, Borachio, Margaret, Ursula, *and others, masked.*

    D. Pedro. Lady, will you walk about with your friend?

    Hero. So you walk softly, and look sweetly, and say
        nothing,

                                  C

I am yours for a walk; and especially when
I walk away.

  D. Pedro. With me in your company?

  Hero. I may say so, when I please.

  D. Pedro.   And when please you to say so?

  Hero. When I like your favour; for God defend
        The lute should be like the case!

  D. Pedro. My visor is Philemon's roof; within the house
    is Jove.

  Hero. Why then your visor should be thatched.

  D. Pedro.   Speak low, if you speak love.
            [Takes her aside.

  Balth. Well, I would you did like me.

  Marg.   So would not I,
For your own sake; for I have many ill qualities.

  Balth. Which is one?

  Marg.   I say my prayers aloud.

  Balth. I love you the better; the hearers may cry Amen.

  Marg. God match me with a good dancer!

  Balth.   Amen.

  Marg. And God keep him out of my sight when the
    dance is done!—
Answer, clerk!

  Balth. No more words: the clerk is answered.

  Urs. I know you well enough; you are Signior Antonio.

  Ant.   At a word, I am not.

  Marg. I know you by the waggling of your head.

  Ant.   To tell you true, I counterfeit him.

  Marg. You could never do him so ill—well, unless
       You were the very man:
Here's his dry hand up and down; you are he, you are he.

  Ant. At a word, I am not.

  Urs.   Come, come, do you think
I do not know you by your excellent wit?
Can virtue hide itself? Go to, mum; you are he:
Graces will appear, and there's an end.

Beat. Will you not tell me who told you so ?

Bene.   No, you shall pardon me.

Beat. Nor will you not tell me who you are ?

Bene.   Not now.

Beat. That I was disdainful, and that I had my good wit

Out of the "Hundred Merry Tales."—Well, this was Signior

Benedick that said so.

Bene.   What's he ?

Beat.   I am sure

You know him well enough.

Bene.   Not I, believe me.

Beat. Did he never make you laugh ?

Bene.   I pray you, what is he ?

Beat. Why he's the prince's jester ; a very dull fool ;

Only his gift is in devising impossible

Slanders : none but libertines delight in him ;

And the commendation is not in his wit, but in

His villainy ; for he both pleases men and angers them ;

And then they laugh at him, and beat him.   I am sure

He is in the fleet : I would he had boarded me.

Bene. When I know the gentleman I'll tell him what
      you say.

Beat. Do, do : he'll but break a comparison or two on
      me ;

Which, peradventure, not marked, or not laughed at,

Strikes him into melancholy ; and then there's a partridge
      wing saved,

For the fool will eat no supper that night.   We must
      follow

The leaders.   [*Music within.*

Bene.   In every good thing.

Beat.   Nay, if they lead

To any ill, I will leave them at the next turning.

> [*Dance : then exeunt all but* Don John,
>   Borachio, *and* Claudio.

D. John. Sure my brother is amorous on Hero, and hath
Withdrawn her father to break with him about it.
The ladies follow her, and but one visor remains.

Bora. And that is Claudio: I know him by his bearing.

D. John. Are you not Signior Benedick?

Claud.   You know me well;
I am he.

D. John. Signior, you are very near my brother
In his love: he is enamoured on Hero; I pray you,
Dissuade him from her; she is no equal for
His birth: you may do the part of an honest man in it.

Claud. How know you he loves her?

D. John.   I heard him swear his affection.

Bora. So did I too; and he swore he would marry her
To-night.

D. John. Come, let us to the banquet.

                    [*Exeunt* DON JOHN *and* BORACHIO.

Claud. Thus answer I in name of Benedick,
But hear these ill news with the ears of Claudio.
'Tis certain so:—the prince woos for himself.
Friendship is constant in all other things,
Save in the office and affairs of love;
Therefore, all hearts in love use their own tongues;
Let every eye negotiate for itself,
And trust no agent; for beauty is a witch,
Against whose charms faith melteth into blood:
This is an accident of hourly proof, which
I mistrusted not.   Farewell, therefore, Hero!

Re-enter BENEDICK.

Bene. Count Claudio?

Claud.   Yea, the same.

Bene.   Come, will you go with me?

Claud.   Whither?

Bene. Even to the next willow, about your own business,
    Count.
What fashion will you wear the garland of it?
About your neck, like an usurer's chain? or under
Your arm, like a lieutenant's scarf?   You must wear it
One way, for the prince hath got your Hero.
    Claud. I wish him joy of her.
    Bene.   Why, that's spoken like
An honest drover; so they sell bullocks.   But did you
Think the prince would have served you thus?
    Claud.   I pray you,
Leave me.
    Bene.   Ho! now you strike like the blind man;
'Twas the boy that stole your meat, and you'll beat the post.
    Claud.   If it will not be, I leave you.
                                    [*Exit.*

    Bene. Alas, poor hurt fowl! now will he creep into
        sedges.—
But that my lady Beatrice should know me, and
Not know me!   The prince's fool!—Ha! it may be,
I go under that title, because I am merry—
Yea; but so, I am apt to do myself wrong:
I am not so reputed: it is nought but
The bitter disposition of Beatrice,
That puts the world into her person, and so
Gives me out.   Well, I'll be revenged as I may.

    D. Pedro. Now, Signior, where's the Count?   Did you see
        him?
    Bene.   Troth,
My lord, I have played the part of lady Fame;
I found him here as melancholy as a lodge in a warren;
I told him, and I think I told him true,
That your grace had got the good will of this young lady;
And I offered him my company to a willow tree,
Either to make him a garland, as being forsaken,
Or to bind him up a rod, as being worthy to be whipped.

D. Pedro. To be whipped! What's his fault?

Bene. The flat transgression
Of a schoolboy; who, being overjoyed with finding
A bird's nest, shows it his companion, and he steals it.

　D. Pedro. Wilt thou make a trust a transgression? The
　　　transgression
Is in the stealer.

Bene. Yet it had not been amiss
The rod had been made and the garland too; for the
　　　garland,
He might have worn it himself; and the rod he might
Have bestow'd on you, who, as I take it, have stolen
His bird's nest.

　D. Pedro. I will but teach them to sing, and restore
　　　them
To the owner.

Bene. If their singing answer your saying,
By my faith, you say honestly.

　D. Pedro. The lady Beatrice
Hath a quarrel to you: the gentleman that danced with
　　　her
Told her she is much wronged by you.

Bene. O, she misused me
Past the endurance of a block! an oak
But with one green leaf on it would have answered her;
My very visor began to assume life and scold with her.
She told me, not thinking I had been myself,
That I was the prince's jester, and that I was duller than
A great thaw; huddling jest upon jest, with such
Impossible conveyance, upon me, that I stood
Like a man at a mark, with a whole army shooting at me.
She speaks poniards, and every word stabs: if her
Breath were as terrible as her terminations,
There were no living near her; she would infect
To the north star. I would not marry her,
Though she were endowed with all that Adam had left him

Before he transgressed: she would have made Hercules
Have turned spit; yea, and have cleft his club
To make the fire too.   Come talk not of her; you shall
    find her
The infernal Até in good apparel.   I would
To God, some scholar would conjure her; for certainly,
While she is here, a man may live as quiet
In hell as in a sanctuary; and people sin upon purpose,
Because they would go thither; so indeed, all disquiet,
Horror, and perturbation, follow her.

Enter CLAUDIO, BEATRICE, HERO, *and* LEONATO.

   D. Pedro. Look, here she comes.
   Bene.   Will your grace command me any service
To the world's end?   I will go on the slightest errand now
To the Antipodes, that you can devise to send me on;
I will fetch you a tooth-picker now from the furthest inch
Of Asia; bring you the length of Prester John's foot;
Fetch you a hair off the great Cham's beard; do you any
                 Embassage to the Pigmies, rather
Than hold three words conference with this harpy.
You have no employment for me?
   D. Pedro.   None, but to desire your
Good company.
   Bene.   O God, sir, here's a dish I love not;
I cannot endure my lady Tongue.   [*Exit.*
   D. Pedro.   Come lady, come;
You have lost the heart of Signior Benedick.
   Beat.   Indeed, my lord,
He lent it me awhile; and I gave him use for it,—
A double heart for his single one: marry, once before,
He won it of me with false dice; therefore your grace
May well say I have lost it.
   D. Pedro.   You have put him down lady, you
Have put him down.

Beat.   So I would not he should do
Me, my lord, lest I should prove the mother of fools.—
I have brought Count Claudio, whom you sent me to seek.

D. Pedro. Why, how now, Count? wherefore are you sad?

Claud.   Not sad,
My lord.

D. Pedro. How then ? sick ?

Claud.   Neither, my lord.

Beat.   The Count
Is neither sad nor sick, nor merry, nor well ;
But civil, Count,—civil as an orange, and something
Of that jealous complexion.

D. Pedro.   I' faith, lady, I think
Your blazon to be true ; though I'll be sworn if he be so,
His conceit is false.   Here, Claudio, I have wooed
In thy name, and fair Hero is won ; I have broke with her
        father,
And, his good will obtained,—name the day of marriage,
And God give thee joy !

Leon.   Count, take of me my daughter,
And with her my fortunes : his grace hath made the
        match,
And all grace say Amen to it !

Beat.   Speak, Count, 'tis your cue.

Claud. Silence is the perfectest herald of joy : I were
But little happy, if I could say how much.—
Lady, as you are mine, I am yours : I give away
Myself for you, and dote upon the exchange.

Beat.   Speak, cousin ;
Or, if you cannot, stop his mouth with a kiss,
And let him not speak neither.

D. Pedro.   In faith, lady, you have
A merry heart.

Beat.   Yea, my lord ; I thank it, poor fool,
It keeps on the windy side of care.—My cousin
Tells him in his ear that he is in her heart.

Claud. And so she doth, cousin.

Beat.   Good lord, for alliance!—
Thus goes every one to the world but I,
And I am sunburn'd; I may sit in a corner,
And cry, heigh ho! for a husband.

D. Pedro.   Lady Beatrice,
I will get you one.

Beat.   I would rather have one of your father's getting.
Hath your grace ne'er a brother like you?   Your father
Got excellent husbands, if a maid could come by them.

D. Pedro. Will you have me, lady?

Beat.   No, my lord, unless
I might have another for working days: your grace
Is too costly to wear every day.—But I beseech
Your grace, pardon me: I was born to speak all mirth
And no matter.

D. Pedro.   Your silence most offends me,
And to be merry best becomes you; for out of question,
You were born in a merry hour.

Beat.   No sure, my lord,
My mother cried; but then there was a star danced,
And under that I was born.—Cousins, God give you joy!

Leon. Niece, will you look to those things I told you of?

Beat. I cry your mercy, uncle.—By your grace's pardon.

[*Exit.*

D. Pedro. By my troth, a pleasant-spirited lady.

Leon.   There's little
Of the melancholy element in her, my lord.
She is never sad but when she sleeps; and not ever
Sad then; for I have heard my daughter say,
She hath often dreamed of unhappiness,
And waked herself with laughing.

D. Pedro.   She cannot endure
To hear tell of a husband.

Leon.   O, by no means: she mocks all
Her wooers out of suit.

D. Pedro.   She were an excellent wife
For Benedick.

Leon.   O Lord, my lord, if they were
But a week married, they would talk themselves mad.

D. Pedro. Count Claudio, when mean you to go to
church ?

Claud. To-morrow, my lord : Time goes on crutches till
love
Have all his rites.

Leon.   Not till Monday, my dear son,
Which is hence a just seven-night ; and a time too brief,
too,
To have all things answer my mind.

D. Pedro.   Come, you shake the head,
At so long a breathing ; but I warrant thee, Claudio,
The time shall not go dully by us. I will, in the interim,
Undertake one of Hercules' labours ; which is,
To bring Signior Benedick and the Lady Beatrice
Into a mountain of affection, the one with the other.
I would fain have it a match ; and I doubt not but to
fashion it,
If you three will but minister such assistance
As I shall give you direction.

Leon.   My lord, I am for you, though it cost me
Ten nights' watchings.

Claud.   And I too, my lord.

D. Pedro.   And you too, gentle Hero ?

Hero. I will do any modest office, my lord,
To help my cousin to a good husband.

D. Pedro.   And Benedick
Is not the unhopefullest husband that I know.
Thus far can I praise him ; he is of a noble strain,
Of approved valour, and confirmed honesty.
I will teach you how to humour your cousin,
That she shall fall in love with Benedick ; —
And I, with your two helps, will so practise on Benedick,

That in despite of his quick wit and his queasy
Stomach, he shall fall in love with Beatrice.
If we can do this, Cupid is no longer an archer;
His glory shall be ours, for we are the only love-gods.
Go in with me, and I will tell you my drift.

[Exeunt.

SCENE II.—*Another Room in* LEONATO'S *House.*

Enter DON JOHN *and* BORACHIO.

D. John. It is so; the Count Claudio shall marry the
    daughter
Of Leonato.

Bora.   Yea, my lord; but I can cross it.

D. John. Any bar, any cross, any impediment
Will be medicinable to me: I am sick in displeasure
To him; and whatsoever comes athwart his affection,
Ranges evenly with mine. How canst thou cross this
    marriage?

Bora. Not honestly, my lord; but so covertly that no
    dishonesty
Shall appear in me.

D. John.   Show me briefly how.

Bora.   I think I told your lordship,
A year since, how much I am in the favour of Margaret,
The waiting gentlewoman to Hero.

D. John.   I remember.

Bora. I can, at any unseasonable instant of the night,
Appoint her to look out at her lady's chamber-window.

D. John. What life is in that, to be the death of this
    marriage?

Bora.   The poison
Of that lies in you to temper. Go you to the prince, your
    brother;
Spare not to tell him that he hath wronged his honour in
    marrying

The renowned Claudio (whose estimation do you mightily
Hold up) to a contaminated stale, such a one as Hero.

D. John. What proof shall I make of that?

Bora.   Proof enough to misuse
The prince, to vex Claudio, to undo Hero, and kill
    Leonato.
Look you for any other issue?

D. John.   Only to despite them,
I will endeavour anything.

Bora.   Go then; find me a meet hour
To draw Don Pedro and Count Claudio alone:
Tell them that you know Hero loves me; intend
A kind of zeal both to the prince and Claudio,
As,—in love of your brother's honour, who hath made this
    match,
And his friend's reputation, who is thus like to be cozened
    with
The semblance of a maid,—that you have discovered thus.
They will scarcely believe this without trial: offer them
    instances;
Which shall bear no less likelihood than to see me
At her chamber-window; hear me call Margaret, Hero;
Hear Margaret call me Claudio; and bring them to see this
The very night before the intended wedding:
For in the meantime I will so fashion the matter that
    Hero
Shall be absent, and there shall appear such seeming truth
Of Hero's disloyalty, that jealousy shall be called assu-
    rance,
And all the preparation overthrown.

D. John.   Grow this to what
Adverse issue it can, I will put it in practice.
Be cunning in the working of this, and thy fee is
A thousand ducats.

Bora.   Be you constant in the accusation;
    And my cunning shall not shame me.

D. John. I will presently go learn their day of marriage.
[*Exeunt.*

Scene III.—Leonato's *Garden.*

Enter Benedick *and a* Boy.

Bene. Boy,—

Boy.   Signior ?

Bene.   In my chamber-window lies a book ;
Bring it hither to me in the orchard.

Boy.   I am here, already, sir.

Bene. I know that ;—but I would have thee hence, and
here
Again. [*Exit* Boy.]—I do much wonder, that one man,
Seeing how much another man is a fool
When he dedicates his behaviours to love,
Will, after he hath laughed at such shallow follies in
others,
Become the argument of his own scorn
By falling in love : and such a man is Claudio.
I have known when there was no music with him
But the drum and the fife ; and now had he rather hear
The tabor and the pipe : I have known when he would
have walked
Ten mile afoot to see a good armour ; and now will he
Lie ten nights awake, carving the fashion
Of a new doublet. He was wont to speak plain and to
the purpose,
Like an honest man and a soldier ; and now is he turn'd
Orthographer ; his words are a very fantastical banquet,—
Just so many strange dishes. May I be so converted,
And see with these eyes ? I cannot tell ; I think not :
I will not be sworn but love may transform me to an oyster ;
But I'll take my oath on it, till he have made an oyster
of me,
He shall never make me such a fool.   One woman

Is fair,—yet I am well: another is wise,—
Yet I am well: another virtuous,—yet I am well:
But till all graces be in one woman, one woman
Shall not come in my grace. Rich she shall be, that's
        certain ;
Wise, or I'll none ; virtuous, or I'll never cheapen her ;
Fair, or I'll never look on her ; mild, or come not near me ;
Noble, or not I for an angel ; of good discourse,
An excellent musician, and her hair shall be of what colour
It pleases God.—Ha ! the prince and monsieur Love !
I will hide me in the arbour.

> [*Withdraws into the arbour.*

Enter Don Pedro, Leonato, Claudio, *and* Balthazar
        with instrument.

D. Pedro.   Come, shall we hear this music ?
Claud. Yea, my good lord.—How still the evening is,
As hush'd on purpose to grace harmony !
D. Pedro. See you where Benedick hath hid himself ?
Claud. O, very well, my lord : the music ended,
We'll fit the hid fox with a pennyworth.
D. Pedro. Come, Balthazar, we'll hear that song again.
Balth. O, good my lord, tax not so bad a voice
To slander music any more than once.
D. Pedro. It is the witness still of excellency,
To put a strange face on his own perfection :—
I pray thee, sing, and let me woo no more.
Balth. Because you talk of wooing, I will sing ;
Since many a wooer doth commence his suit
To her he thinks not worthy ; yet he woos ;
Yet will he swear, he loves.
D. Pedro.   Nay, pray thee, come ;
Or, if thou wilt hold longer argument,
Do it in notes.
Balth.   Note this before my notes,
There's not a note of mine that's worth the noting.

D. Pedro. Why, these are very crotchets that he speaks;
        Note, notes, forsooth, and noting!   [*Music.*
Bene. [*Aside.*] Now, divine air! now is his soul ravish'd!—
Is it not strange that sheeps' guts should hale souls
Out of men's bodies?—Well, a horn for my money,
When all's done.

BALTHAZAR sings.

I.

Sigh no more, ladies, sigh no more,
    Men were deceivers ever;
One foot in sea, and one on shore:
    To one thing constant never:
        Then sigh not so,
        But let them go,
    And be you blithe and bonny;
Converting all your sounds of woe
    Into, Hey nonny, nonny.

II.

Sing no more ditties, sing no mo
    Of dumps so dull and heavy;
The fraud of men was ever so,
    Since summer first was leavy.
        Then sigh not so, &c.

D. Pedro. By my troth, a good song.
Balth.   And an ill singer, my lord.
D. Pedro. Ha? no, no, faith; thou singest well enough
For a shift.
Bene. [*Aside.*]   An he had been a dog that should
Have howled thus, they would have hanged him: and I
        pray God
His bad voice bode no mischief!   I had as lief have heard
The night raven, come what plague could have come after
        it.

D. Pedro. [*To* CLAUDIO.] Yea, marry.—Dost thou hear,
    Balthazar ? I pray thee
Get us some excellent music for to-morrow night ;
We would have it at the lady Hero's chamber-window.
    Balth. The best I can, my lord.
    D. Pedro.   Do so ; farewell,—

                            [*Exit* BALTHAZAR.

Come hither, Leonato : what was it you told me of
To-day—that your niece Beatrice was in love
With Signior Benedick ?
    Claud. O, ay :—[*Aside to* PEDRO.] Stalk on, stalk on ;
The fowl sits. —[*Aloud.*] I did never think that lady
Would have loved any man.
    Leon.   No, nor I neither ; but most wonderful that
She should so dote on Signior Benedick,
Whom she hath in all outward behaviours
Seemed ever to abhor.
    Bene. [*Aside.*]   Is't possible ?
Sits the wind in that corner ?
    Leon.   By my troth,
My lord, I cannot tell what to think of it ;
But that she loves him with an enraged affection,—
It is past the infinite of thought.
    D. Pedro.   May be she doth
But counterfeit.
    Claud.   Faith, like enough.
    Leon.   O God ! counterfeit !
There was never counterfeit of passion came
So near the life of passion as she discovers it.
    D. Pedro. Why, what effects of passion shows she ?
    Claud. [*Aside.*]   Bait the hook well ;
This fish will bite.
    Leon. What effects, my lord ? She will sit you,—
You heard my daughter tell you how.
    Claud.   She did, indeed.

D. Pedro.   How, how, I pray you ?   You amaze me :
I would have thought her spirits had been invincible
Against all assaults of affection.

Leon.   I would have sworn
It had, my lord ; especially against Benedick.

Bene. [*Aside.*]   I should think this a gull, but that
The white-bearded fellow speaks it : knavery
Cannot, sure, hide himself in such reverence.

Claud. [*Aside.*] He hath ta'en the infection : hold it up.

D. Pedro.   Hath she made
Her affection known to Benedick ?

Leon.   No ; and swears

                    She never will : that's her torment.

Claud. 'Tis true, indeed ; so your daughter says : "Shall
            I,"
Says she, "that have so oft encountered him
With scorn, write to him that I love him ?"

Leon.   This says
She now, when she is beginning to write to him ;
For she'll be up twenty times a night ; and there
Will she sit in her smock till she have writ a sheet
Of paper :—my daughter tells us all.

Claud.   Now you talk of a sheet
Of paper, I remember a pretty jest
Your daughter told us of.

Leon.   O !—when she had writ it,
And was reading it over, she found Benedick
And Beatrice between the sheet !—

Claud.   That.

Leon.   O ! she tore
The letter into a thousand halfpence ; railed at herself,
That she should be so immodest to write to one that
She knew would flout her :
                    "I measure him," says she, " by my own spirit ;
For I should flout him if he writ to me ;
Yea, though I love him, I should."

Claud.   Then down upon
Her knees she falls, weeps, sobs, beats her heart, tears
  her hair, prays;
Cries, "O sweet Benedick! God give me patience!"

Leon. She doth indeed: my daughter says so; and
The ecstasy hath so much overborne her, that
My daughter is sometimes afraid she will do
A desperate outrage to herself: it is very
True.

D. Pedro. It were good that Benedick knew of it, by
Some other, if she will not discover it.

Claud.   To what end?
He would but make a sport of it, and torment
The poor lady worse.

D. Pedro.   An he should, it were an alms
To hang him. She's an excellent sweet lady;
And out of all suspicion, she is virtuous.

Claud. And she is exceeding wise.

D. Pedro.   In everything
But in loving Benedick.

Leon.   O, my lord, wisdom and blood
Combating in so tender a body, we have
Ten proofs to one that blood hath the victory.
I am sorry for her, as I have just cause,
Being her uncle and her guardian,

D. Pedro. I would she had bestowed this dotage on me:
I would have daffed all other respects and made her
Half myself. I pray you, tell Benedick of it,
And hear what he will say.

Leon.   Were it good, think you?

Claud. Hero thinks surely she will die; for she says she
  will die,
If he love her not; and she will die ere she make her love
  known;
And she will die, if he woo her, rather than she
Will bate one breath of her accustomed crossness.

D. Pedro.   She doth
Well; if she should make tender of her love,
'Tis very possible he'll scorn it; for the man,
As you know all, hath a contemptible spirit.

Claud. He is a very proper man.

D. Pedro.   He hath
Indeed a good outward happiness.

Claud.   'Fore God,
And in my mind, very wise.

D. Pedro.   He doth indeed
Show some sparks that are like wit.

Leon.   And I take him
To be valiant.

D. Pedro.   As Hector, I assure you; and in the
Managing of quarrels, you may say he is wise;
For either he avoids them with great discretion,
Or undertakes them with a most Christian-like fear.

Leon. If he do fear God, he must necessarily
Keep peace; if he break the peace he ought to enter into
A quarrel with fear and trembling.

D. Pedro.   And so he will do;
For the man doth fear God, howsoever it seems
Not in him by some large jests he will make.   Well, I am
Sorry for your niece.   Shall we go seek Benedick,
And tell him of her love?

Claud.   Never tell him, my lord;
Let her wear it out with good counsel.

Leon.   Nay, that's impossible;
She may wear her heart out first.

D. Pedro.   Well, we'll hear further of it
By your daughter: let it cool the while.   I love
Benedick well; and I could wish he would modestly
Examine himself, to see how much he is
Unworthy so good a lady.

Leon.   My lord, will you walk?
Dinner is ready.

Claud. [*Aside.*]   If he do not dote on her upon this,
I will never trust my expectation.

    D. Pedro. [*Aside.*]   Let there be
The same net spread for her; and that must your daughter
And her gentlewomen carry.   The sport will be,
When they hold one an opinion of another's dotage,
And no such matter: that's the scene that I would
See, which will be merely a dumb show.   Let us send her
To call him in to dinner.

                    [*Exeunt* DON PEDRO, CLAUDIO, *and* LEONATO.

BENEDICK *advancing from the Arbour.*

    Bene.   This can be no trick ; the conference
Was sadly borne.—They have the truth of this from Hero.
They seem to pity the lady ; it seems her affections
Have their full bent.   Love me ! why it must be requited.
I hear how I am censured: they say I will bear myself
        proudly,
If I perceive the love came from her: they say too,
That she will rather die than give any sign of
Affection.—I did never think to marry : I must not seem
Proud.—Happy are they that hear their detractions, and
Can put them to mending.   They say the lady is fair,—
'Tis a truth, I can bear them witness ; and virtuous,—'tis
        so,
I cannot reprove it; and wise, but for loving me :
By my troth, it is no addition to her wit ;
Nor no great argument of her folly ; for I
Will be horribly in love with her.   I may chance have
        some odd
Quirks and remnants of wit broken on me, because
I have railed so long against marriage :—but doth not the
        appetite
Alter ?   A man loves the meat in his youth that
He cannot endure in his age.   Shall quips, sentences, and

These paper bullets of the brain, awe a man from
The career of his humour? No; the world must
Be peopled. When I said I would die a bachelor,
I did not think I should live till I were married.—
Here comes Beatrice. By this day, she's a fair lady:
I do spy some marks of love in her.

Enter BEATRICE.

Beat.   Against my will
I am sent to bid you come in to dinner.
Bene.   Fair Beatrice,
I thank you for your pains.
Beat.   I took no more pains for
Those thanks than you took pains to thank me: if it had
Been painful, I would not have come.
Bene.   You took pleasure, then,
In the message?
Beat.   Yea, so much as you may take
Upon a knife's point, and choke a daw withal.—
You have no stomach, signior? fare you well.   [*Exit.*
Bene. Ha! "Against my will I am sent to bid you come
        in
To dinner,"—there's a double meaning in that. "I took
        no more
Pains for those thanks than you took pains to thank me,"—
That's as much as to say, Any pains that I take for
You, is as easy as thanks.—If I do not take pity of her,
I am a villain; if I do not love her,
I am a Jew: I will go get her picture.
                                            [*Exit.*

ACT III.

SCENE I.—LEONATO'S *Garden.*

Enter HERO, MARGARET, *and* URSULA.

Hero.

GOOD Margaret, run thee to the parlour;
    There shall thou find my cousin Beatrice
    Proposing with the prince and Claudio:
Whisper her ear, and tell her, I and Ursula
Walk in the orchard, and our whole discourse
Is all of her: say that thou overheard'st us;
And bid her steal into the pleachèd bower,
Where honeysuckles, ripen'd by the sun,
Forbid the sun to enter;—like favourites,
Made proud by princes, that advance their pride
Against that power that bred it:—there will she hide her,
To listen our propose. This is thy office,
Bear thee well in it, and leave us alone.

   Marg. I'll make her come, I warrant you, presently.

                                 [*Exit.*

   Hero. Now, Ursula, when Beatrice doth come,
As we do trace this alley up and down,
Our talk must only be of Benedick.
When I do name him, let it be thy part
To praise him more than ever man did merit:
My talk to thee must be, how Benedick
Is sick in love with Beatrice. Of this matter
Is little Cupid's crafty arrow made,
That only wounds by hearsay.

          Enter BEATRICE, *behind.*

                 Now begin
For look where Beatrice, like a lapwing, runs
Close by the ground, to hear our conference.

Urs. The pleasant'st angling is to see the fish
Cut with their golden oars the silver stream,
And greedily devour the treacherous bait:
So angle we for Beatrice; who even now
Is couchèd in the woodbine coverture.
Fear you not my part of the dialogue.

Hero. Then go we near her, that her ear lose nothing
Of the false sweet bait, that we lay for it.—

[*They advance to the bower.*

No, truly, Ursula, she is too disdainful;
I know her spirits are as coy and wild
As haggards of the rock.

Urs.   But are you sure
That Benedick loves Beatrice so entirely?

Hero. So says the prince, and my new-trothèd lord.

Urs. And did they bid you tell her of it, madam?

Hero. They did entreat me to acquaint her of it;
But I persuaded them, if they lov'd Benedick,
To wish him wrestle with affection,
And never to let Beatrice know of it.

Urs. Why did you so?   Doth not the gentleman
Deserve as full, as fortunate a bed,
As ever Beatrice shall couch upon?

Hero. O God of love!   I know he doth deserve
As much as may be yielded to a man:
But nature never fram'd a woman's heart
Of prouder stuff than that of Beatrice;
Disdain and scorn ride sparkling in her eyes,
Misprising what they look on; and her wit
Values itself so highly, that to her
All matter else seems weak.   She cannot love,
Nor take no shape nor project of affection,
She is so self-endeared.

Urs.   Sure I think so;
And therefore, certainly, it were not good
She knew his love, lest she make sport at it.

Hero. Why, you speak truth.   I never yet saw man,
How wise, how noble, young, how rarely featur'd,
But she would spell him backward: if fair-faced,
She'd swear the gentleman should be her sister ;
If black, why, nature, drawing of an antic,
Made a foul blot ; if tall, a lance ill-headed ;
If low, an agate very vilely cut ;
If speaking, why a vane blown with all winds ;
If silent, why a block movèd with none.
So turns she every man the wrong side out ;
And never gives to truth and virtue that
Which simpleness and merit purchaseth.

Urs. Sure, sure, such carping is not commendable.

Hero. No ; not to be so odd, and from all fashions,
As Beatrice is, cannot be commendable :
But who dare tell her so ?   If I should speak,
She'd mock me into air : O, she would laugh me
Out of myself, press me to death with wit !
Therefore let Benedick, like cover'd fire,
Consume away in sighs, waste inwardly :
It were a better death than die with mocks,
Which is as bad as die with tickling.

Urs. Yet tell her of it : hear what she will say.

Hero. No ; rather I will go to Benedick,
And counsel him to fight against his passion :
And, truly, I'll devise some honest slanders
To stain my cousin with : one doth not know
How much an ill word may empoison liking.

Urs. O, do not do your cousin such a wrong !
She cannot be so much without true judgment,
(Having so swift and excellent a wit,
As she is priz'd to have) as to refuse
So rare a gentleman as Signior Benedick.

Hero. He is the only man of Italy,
Always excepted my dear Claudio.

Urs. I pray you, be not angry with me, madam

Speaking my fancy: Signior Benedick,
For shape, for bearing, argument, and valour,
Goes foremost in report through Italy.

Hero. Indeed, he hath an excellent good name.

Urs. His excellency did earn it, ere he had it.—
When are you married, madam?

Hero.   Why, every day—to-morrow.   Come, go in:
I'll show thee some attires; and have thy counsel,
Which is the best to furnish me to-morrow.

Urs. [*Aside.*]   She's lim'd, I warrant you: we have
    caught her, madam.

Hero. [*Aside.*]   If it prove so, then loving goes by haps:
Some Cupid kills with arrows, some with traps.

[*Exeunt* HERO *and* URSULA.

BEATRICE *advances.*

Beat. What fire is in mine ears?   Can this be true?
    Stand I condemn'd for pride and scorn so much?
Contempt, farewell! and maiden pride, adieu!
    No glory lives behind the back of such.
And, Benedick, love on: I will requite thee,
    Taming my wild heart to thy loving hand.
If thou dost love, my kindness shall incite thee
    To bind our loves up in a holy band;
For others say thou dost deserve, and I
Believe it better than reportingly.   [*Exit.*

SCENE II.—*A Room in* LEONATO'S *House.*

Enter DON PEDRO, CLAUDIO, BENEDICK, *and* LEONATO.

D. Pedro. I do but stay till your marriage be consum-
    mate,
And then go I toward Arragon.

Claud.   I'll bring you
Thither, my lord, if you'll vouchsafe me.

D. Pedro.   Nay,
That would be as great a soil
        In the new gloss of your marriage as to show
A child his new coat and forbid him to wear it.
I will only be bold with Benedick for his company;
For from the crown of his head to the sole of his foot,
He is all mirth:
        He hath twice or thrice cut Cupid's bowstring, and
The little hangman dare not shoot at him; he hath
A heart as sound as a bell, and his tongue is the clapper;
For what his heart thinks, his tongue speaks.

Bene.   Gallants,
I am not as I have been.

Leon.   So say I;
Methinks you are sadder.

Claud.   I hope he be in love.

D. Pedro. Hang him, truant! there's no true drop of
        blood in him,
To be truly touched with love: if he be sad,
He wants money.

Bene.   I have the toothache.

D. Pedro.   Draw it.

Bene.   Hang it!

Claud. You must hang it first and draw it afterwards.

D. Pedro. What! sigh for the toothache?

Leon.   Where is but a humour, or a worm.

Bene. Well, every man can master a grief, but he
That has it.

Claud.   Yet say I, he is in love.

D. Pedro. There is no appearance of fancy in him, unless
It is a fancy that he hath to strange disguises;
As to be a Dutchman to-day, a Frenchman to-morrow;
Or in the shape of two countries at once;
As a German from the waist downward, all slops;
And a Spaniard from the hip upward, no doublet.
Unless he hath a fancy to this foolery,

As it appears he hath, he is no fool
For fancy, as you would have it appear he is.
    Claud.   If he be not
In love with some woman, there is no believing old signs :
He brushes his hat o' mornings ; what should that bode ?
    D. Pedro. Hath any man seen him at the barber's ?
    Claud.   No,
But the barber's man hath been seen with him ; and the
        old
Ornament of his cheek hath already stuffed tennis-balls.
    Leon. Indeed, he looks younger than he did, by the loss
        of a beard.
    D. Pedro. Nay, a' rubs himself with civet : can you smell
        him out by that ?
    Claud. That's as much as to say the sweet youth 's in
        love.
    D. Pedro. The greatest note of it is his melancholy.
    Claud. And when was he wont to wash his face ?
    D. Pedro.   Yea, or to
Paint himself ? for the which, I hear what they say of
        him.
    Claud. Nay, but his jesting spirit ; which is now crept
Into a lutestring, and now governed by stops.
    D. Pedro. Indeed, that tells a heavy tale for him. Con-
        clude,
Conclude he is in love.
    Claud.   Nay, but I know
Who loves him.
    D. Pedro.   That would I know too ; I warrant
One that knows him not.
    Claud.   Yes, and his ill conditions ;
And in despite of all, dies for him.
    D. Pedro.   She shall be buried
With her face upwards.
    Bene.   Yet is this no charm
For the toothache.—Old signior, walk aside with me :

I have studied eight or nine wise words to speak
To you, which these hobby-horses must not hear.

       [*Exeunt* BENEDICK *and* LEONATO.

D. Pedro. For my life, to break with him about Beatrice.

Claud. 'Tis even so. Hero and Margaret
Have by this played their parts with Beatrice ;
And then the two bears will not bite one another

          When they meet.

     Enter DON JOHN.

D. John. My lord and brother, God save you.

D. Pedro.   Good den, brother.

D. John. If your leisure served, I would speak with you.

D. Pedro.   In private ?

D. John. If it please you : yet Count Claudio may hear,
   for what I
Would speak of concerns him.

D. Pedro.   What's the matter ?

D. John. [*To* CLAUDIO.]   Means
Your lordship to be married to-morrow ?

D. Pedro.   You know he does.

D. John. I know not that, when he knows what I know.

Claud.   If
There be any impediment, I pray you discover it.

D. John. You may think I love you not : let that appear
   hereafter,
And aim better at me by that I now will manifest.
For my brother, I think, he holds you well ; and in dear-
   ness
Of heart hath holp to effect your ensuing marriage,—
Surely suit ill-spent and labour ill-bestowed.

D. Pedro. Why, what's the matter ?

D. John.   I came hither to tell you ;
And circumstances shortened (for she hath been too long
A talking of), the lady is disloyal.

Claud.   Who ? Hero ?

D. John. Even she : Leonato's Hero ; your Hero ; every
  man's
Hero.

Claud. Disloyal ?

D. John.   The word is too good to paint out
Her wickedness : I could say she were worse ; think you
Of a worse title and I will fit her to it.
Wonder not till further warrant : go but with me to-night,
You shall see her chamber-window entered, even the
Night before her wedding-day : if you love her then,
To-morrow wed her ; but it would better fit your honour
To change your mind.

Claud.   May this be so ?

D. Pedro.   I will not think it.

D. John. If you dare not trust that you see, confess not
  that you know.
If you will follow me, I will show you enough ; and when
You have seen more, and heard more, proceed accordingly.

Claud. If I see anything to-night why I should not
  marry her to-morrow,
In the congregation, where I should wed, there will I
  shame her.

D. Pedro. And as I wooed for thee to obtain her, I will
  join with thee
To disgrace her.

D. John.   I will disparage her no farther till you
Are my witnesses : bear it but coldly till midnight,
And let the issue show itself.

D. Pedro.   O day
Untowardly turned !

Claud.   O mischief, strangely thwarting !

D. John. O plague right well prevented !
So will you say when you have seen the sequel.

                                        [*Exeunt.*

SCENE III.—*Night.—A Street.*

Enter DOGBERRY *and* VERJUICE, *with the* WATCH.

Dogb. Are you good men and true?

Verj.   Yea, or else it were pity
But they should suffer salvation, body and soul.

Dogb. Nay that punishment were too good for them
If they should have any allegiance in them, being chosen
For the prince's watch.

Verj. Well, give them their charge, neighbour Dogberry.

Dogb. First, who think you the most desartless man to
  be constable?

Watch. Hugh Oatcake, sir, or George Seacoal; for they
Can write and read.

Dogb.   Come hither, neighbour Seacoal.
God hath blessed you with a good name; to be
A well-favoured man is the gift of fortune;
But to read and write comes by nature.

Seacoal.   Both which, master constable,—

Dogb. You have; I knew it would be your answer. Well,
For your favour, sir, give God thanks, and make no boast
  of it;
And for your writing and reading, let that appear
                    When there is no need for such vanity.
You are thought to be the most senseless and fit man
For the constable of the watch; therefore bear you the
  lantern.
This is your charge:—you shall comprehend all vagrom
  men:
You are to bid any man stand in the prince's name.

Seacoal. How if a' will not stand?

Dogb.   Why then take no note of him, but
Let him go; and presently call the rest of the watch
Together, and thank God you are rid of a knave.

Verj. If he will not stand when he is bidden, he is none
Of the prince's subjects.

Dogb.   True, and they are to meddle
With none but the prince's subjects.—You shall also
Make no noise in the streets; for, for the watch to
Babble and talk is most tolerable and not to be endured.

    Watch. We will rather sleep than talk; we know what
        belongs
To a watch.

    Dogb.   Why, you speak like an ancient and quiet
        watchman;
For I cannot see how sleeping should offend: only have a
        care
That your bills be not stolen.—Well, you are to call at all
The ale-houses, and bid those that are drunk get them to bed.

    Seacoal. How, if they will not?

    Dogb.   Why then let them alone till they are sober;
If they make you not then the better answer, you may—
Say they are not the men you took them for.

    Seacoal.   Well, sir?

    Dogb. If you meet a thief you may suspect him,
By virtue of your office, to be no true man;
And for such kind of men, the less you meddle or
Make with them, why, the more is for your honesty.

    Watch. If we know him to be a thief shall we not lay
        hands on him?

    Dogb. Truly, by your office you may; but I think they
        that touch
Pitch will be defiled;
        The most peaceable way for you, if you do
        take a thief, is
To let him show himself what he is, and steal out of your
        company.

    Verj. You have been always called a merciful man,
        partner.

    Dogb. Truly, I would not hang a dog by my will; much
        more
A man, who hath any honesty in him.

Verj.   If you
Hear a child cry in the night, you must call to the nurse,
And bid her still it.

Seacoal.   How if the nurse be asleep
And will not hear us ?

Dogb.   Why then depart in peace,
And let the child wake her with crying;
For the ewe that will not hear her lamb when it baes,
Will never answer a calf when he bleats.

Verj.   'Tis very
True.

Dogb.   This is the end of the charge.—You, constable,
Are to present the prince's own person : if you meet
The prince in the night, you may stay him.

Verj.   Nay, by 'r lady,
That I think a' cannot.

Dogb.   Five shillings to one on 't,
With any man that knows the statues, he may stay him :
Marry, not without the prince be willing, for indeed
The watch ought to offend no man ; and it is an offence
To stay a man against his will.

Verj.   By 'r lady, I think it be so.

Dogb. Ha, ha, ha ! Well, masters, good-night : an there be
Any matter of weight chances, call up me :
Keep your fellows' counsels and your own ! and good
        night.—

                                        Come, neighbour.

Seacoal. Well, masters, we hear our charge : let us go sit
        here
Upon the church-bench till two, and then all to bed.

Dogb. One word more, honest neighbours : I pray you,
        watch
About Signior Leonato's door ; for the wedding being there
To-morrow, there is a great coil to-night.   Adieu,
                        Be vigitant, I beseech you.
                [Exeunt DOGBERRY *and* VERJUICE.

Enter BORACHIO *and* CONRADE.

Bora. What, Conrade!

Seacoal. [Aside.]   Peace! stir not.

Bora.   Conrade, I say!

Con.   Here man, I am at thy elbow.

Bora. Mass, and my elbow itched; I thought there
     would
A scab follow.

Con.   I will owe thee an answer for that;
And now forward with thy tale.

Bora.   Stand thee close, then,
Under this penthouse, for it drizzles rain;
And I will, like a true drunkard, utter all to thee.

Seacoal. [Aside.] Some treason, masters; yet stand close.

Bora.   Therefore know
I have earned of Don John a thousand ducats.

Con. Is it possible that any villainy should be
So dear?

Bora.   Thou shouldst rather ask, if it were possible
Any villainy should be so rich; for when rich villains
Have need of poor ones, poor ones may make what price
They will.

Con.   I wonder at it.

Bora.   That shows thou art unconfirmed.
Thou knowest that the fashion of a doublet, or a hat,
Or a cloak is nothing to a man.

Con.   Yes, it is apparel.

Bora.   Tush!
I may as well say the fool's the fool.   But seest thou not
What a deformed thief this fashion is?

Watch. I know that Deformed; a' has been a vile thief
     this seven year:
A' goes up and down like a gentleman: I remember his
     name.

Bora. Didst thou not hear somebody?

                                          E

Con.   No; 'twas the vane on the house.

Bora. Seest thou not, I say, what a deformed thief
This fashion is? how giddily a' turns about all
The hot bloods between fourteen and five-and-thirty?
Sometime, fashioning them like Pharaoh's soldiers
In the reechy painting; sometime, like god Bel's priests
In the old church window; sometime, like the shaven
          Hercules,
In the smirched worm-eaten tapestry, where his cod-piece
Seems as massy as his club?

Con.   All this I see; and see
That the fashion wears out more apparel than the man.
          But art not
Thou thyself giddy with the fashion too, that thou hast
          shifted
Out of thy tale into telling me of the fashion?

Bora. Not so neither: but know, that I have to-night
Wooed Margaret, the lady Hero's gentlewoman,
By the name of Hero; she leans me out of her mistress'
Chamber-window; bids me a thousand times
Good night.—I tell this tale vilely:—I should first tell
          thee
How the prince, Claudio, and my master, planted
And placed and possessed by my master, Don John,
Saw afar off in the orchard this amiable
Encounter.

Con.   And thought they, Margaret was Hero?

Bora. Two of them did, the Prince and Claudio;
But the devil my master knew she was Margaret;
And partly by his oaths, which first possessed them,
Partly by the dark night, which did deceive them,
But chiefly by my villainy, which did
Confirm any slander that Don John had made,
Away went Claudio enraged; swore he would meet her,
As he was appointed, next morning at the temple,
And there, before the whole congregation, shame her

With what he saw over-night, and send her home again
Without a husband.

 Watch. We charge you in the prince's name, stand.

 Seacoal. Call up the right master constable : we have
   here recovered
The most dangerous piece of lechery that ever was known
In the commonwealth.

 Watch.   And one Deformed is one of them ; I
   know him,
He wears a lock.

 Con. Masters, masters !

 Watch.   You'll be made to bring Deformed
Forth, I warrant you.

 Con.   Masters !—

 Seacoal.   Never speak we charge you,
Let us obey you to go with us.

 Bora.   We are likely to prove a goodly
Commodity, being taken up of these men's bills.

 Con. A commodity in question, I warrant you. Come,
   we'll obey you.   *[Exeunt.*

SCENE IV.—*A Room in* LEONATO'S *House.*

Enter HERO, MARGARET, *and* URSULA.

 Hero. Good Ursula, wake my cousin Beatrice, and
Desire her to rise.

 Urs. I will, lady.

 Hero.   And bid her come hither.

 Urs.   Well.
        [Exit URSULA.

 Marg. Troth, I think your other rabato were better.

 Hero.   No pray thee,
Good Meg, I'll wear this.

 Marg.   By my troth's not so good ;
And I warrant your cousin will say so.

        E 2

Hero.   My cousin's a fool,
And thou art another; I'll wear none but this.
  Marg. I like the new tire within excellently,
If the hair were a thought browner: and your gown's
A most rare fashion, i' faith; I saw the Duchess
Of Milan's gown that they praise so.
  Hero.   O, that exceeds, they say.
  Marg. By my troth's but a night gown in respect
Of yours: cloth of gold and cuts and laced with silver;
Set with pearls down sleeves; side sleeves and skirts
      round
Underborne with a blueish tinsel; but for a
Fine, quaint, graceful, and excellent fashion,
Yours is worth ten on't.
  Hero.   God give me joy to wear it,
For my heart is exceeding heavy.
  Marg.   'Twill be heavier soon
By the weight of a man.
  Hero.   Fie upon thee! art not ashamed?
  Marg. Of what, lady? of speaking honourably?
Is not marriage honourable in a beggar?
Is not your lord honourable without marriage?
I think you would have me say,—"saving your reverence,—
A husband:" an bad thinking do not wrest true speaking,
I'll offend nobody. Is there any harm in—
"The heavier for a husband"? None, I think, an it be
The right husband and the right wife; otherwise,
'Tis light and not heavy; ask my lady Beatrice else:
Here she comes.

Enter BEATRICE.

  Hero.   Good-morrow, coz.
  Beat.   Good-morrow, sweet Hero.
  Hero. Why, how now! do you speak in the sick tune?
  Beat.   I am out of
All other tune, methinks.

Marg.   Clap us into—" Light o' love ; "
That goes without a burden ; do you sing it,
And I'll dance it.

Beat.   Yea, Light o' love with your heels ?—
Then if your husband have stables enough, you'll see
He shall lack no barns.

Marg.   O illegitimate
Construction ! I scorn that with my heels.

Beat. 'Tis almost five o'clock, cousin ; 'tis time you were
     ready.
By my troth, I am exceeding ill : heigh-ho !

Marg.   For a hawk,
A horse, or a husband ?

Beat.   For the letter that begins
Them all, H.

Marg.   Well, an you be not turned Turk,
There's no more sailing by the star.

Beat.   What means the fool, trow ?

Marg. Nothing I ; but God send every one
                              Their heart's desire !

Hero. These gloves the Count sent me ; they are an
     excellent
Perfume.

Beat.   I am stuffed, cousin ; I cannot smell.

Marg. A maid and stuffed ! there's goodly catching of
     cold.

Beat. O, God help me ! God help me ! How long have you
Professed apprehension ?

Marg.   Ever since you left it :
Doth not my wit become me rarely ?

Beat.   It is not
Seen enough ; you should wear it in your cap.—
By my troth, I am sick.

Marg.   Get you some of this
Distilled Carduus benedictus, and lay it
To your heart : it is the only thing for a qualm.

Hero. There thou prick'st her with a thistle.

Beat.   Benedictus!
Why benedictus? You have some moral in this
Benedictus.

Marg.   Moral? no by my troth, I have
No moral meaning; I meant plain holy-thistle.
You may think, perchance, that I think you are in love:
Nay, by'r lady, I am not such a fool to think
What I list; nor I list not to think what I can; nor indeed,
I cannot think, if I would think my heart out of thinking,
That you are in love, or that you will be in love, or
That you can be in love: yet Benedick was
Such another, and now is he become a man: he swore
He would never marry; and yet now, in despite of his
        heart,
He eats his meat without grudging: and how you
May be converted, I know not; but methinks,
You look with your eyes, as other women do.

Beat.   What pace
Is this that thy tongue keeps?

Mary.   Not a false gallop.

Re-enter URSULA.

Urs.   Madam,
Withdraw; the prince, the count, Signior Benedick, Don
        John,
And all the gallants of the town are come
To fetch you to church.

Hero.   Help to dress me, good coz, good Meg,
        good Ursula.

                                    [*Exeunt.*

Scene V.—*Another Room in* Leonato's *House.*

Enter Leonato *with* Dogberry *and* Verjuice.

Leon. What would you with me, honest neighbour ?

Dogb.   Marry, sir.
I would have some confidence with you, that decerns you
    nearly.

Leon. Brief, I pray you ; for you see, it is a busy time
    with me.

Dogb. Marry, this it is, sir.

Verj.   Yes, in truth it is, sir.

Leon.   What is it, my good friends ?

Dogb. Goodman Verjuice, sir, speaks a little off the
    matter :
An old man, sir, and his wits are not so blunt,
As, God help, I would desire they were ; but, in faith,
Honest as the skin between his brows.

Verj.   Yes, I thank God,
I am as honest as any man living, that is an old man,
And none honester than I.

Dogb.   Comparisons are odorous : *palabras,*
Neighbour Verjuice.

Leon.   Neighbours, you are tedious.

Dogb.   It pleases your worship
To say so ; but we are the poor duke's officers ; but truly,
For mine own part, if I were as tedious as a king, I could
Find in my heart to bestow it all of your worship.

Leon.   All thy
Tediousness on me, ha ?

Dogb.   Yea, an 'twere a thousand pound more than 'tis ;
For I hear as good exclamation on your worship as of any
    man
In the city ; and though I be but a poor man, I am
Glad to hear it.

Verj.   And so am I.

Leon.   I would fain know what you have to say.

Verj. Marry, sir, our watch to-night, excepting your
     worship's presence,

Have ta'en a couple of as arrant knaves as any in Messina.

Dogb. A good old man, sir; he will be talking:

         As they say, when the age is in,

The wit is out. God help us! it is a world to see!—

Well said, i' faith, neighbour Verjuice!—well, God's a
     good man;

An two men ride of a horse, one must ride behind.—An
     honest

Soul i' faith, sir! by my troth he is, as ever broke bread; but
God is to be worshipped.

     All men are not alike;—alas, good neighbour!

Leon. Indeed, neighbour, he comes too short of you.

Dogb. Gifts, that God gives.

Leon.   I must leave you.

Dogb.   One word, sir; our watch, sir,

Hath indeed comprehended two aspicious persons, and

We would have them this morning examined before your
     worship.

Leon. Take their examination yourself, and bring it me;
I am now in great haste, as it may appear unto you.

Dogb. It shall be suffigance.

Leon.   Drink some wine ere you go. Fare you well.

Enter a MESSENGER.

Mess. My lord, they stay for you to give your daughter
To her husband.

Leon.   I will wait upon them; I am ready.

         [*Exeunt* LEONATO *and* MESSENGER.

Dogb. Go, good partner, go; get you to Francis Seacoal.
Bid him bring his pen and inkhorn to the gaol: we are now

To examination these men.

    Verj.   And we must do it wisely.

    Dogb. We will spare for no wit, I warrant you ; here's

       that

Shall drive some of them to a *non com :* only get

The learned writer to set down our excommunication,

                  And meet me at the gaol.

                         [*Exeunt.*

ACT IV.

SCENE I.—*The Inside of a Church.*

Enter DON PEDRO, DON JOHN, LEONATO, FRIAR FRANCIS,
CLAUDIO, BENEDICK, HERO, *and others.*

Leonato.

OME, friar Francis, be brief;
    Only to the plain form of marriage,
    And you shall recount their particular duties
    afterwards.

Friar. You come hither, my lord, to marry this lady ?

Claud.   No.

Leon. To be married to her, friar ; you come to marry her.

Friar. Lady, you come hither to be married to the Count ?

Hero. I do.

Friar.   If either of you know any inward impediment,
Why you should not be conjoined, I charge you on
Your souls to utter it.

Claud.   Know you any, Hero ?

Hero.   None, my lord.

Friar. Know you any, Count ?

Leon.   I dare make his answer,—None.

Claud. O what men dare do ! what men may do ! what
    men daily do !
Not knowing what they do !

Bene.   How now ! Interjections ?
Why then, some be of laughing, as ha ! ha ! he !

Claud. Stand thee by, friar.—Father, by your leave :
Will you with free and unconstrainèd soul
Give me this maid, your daughter ?

Leon.   As freely, son, as God did give her me.

Claud. And what have I to give you back, whose worth
May counterpoise this rich and precious gift ?

D. Pedro. Nothing, unless you render her again.

Claud. Sweet prince, you learn me noble thankfulness.—
There, Leonato, take her back again :
Give not this rotten orange to your friend ;
She's but the sign and semblance of her honour.—
Behold, how like a maid she blushes here !
O, what authority, and show of truth
Can cunning sin cover itself withal !
Comes not that blood, as modest evidence,
To witness simple virtue ? Would you not swear,
All you that see her, that she were a maid,
By these exterior shows ?—But she is none :
She knows the heat of a luxurious bed ;
Her blush is guiltiness, not modesty.

Leon. What do you mean, my lord ?

Claud.   Not to be married ; not to knit my soul
To an approved wanton.

Leon.   Dear my lord,
If you in your own proof
                    Have vanquished the resistance of her youth
And made defeat of her virginity,—

Claud. I know what you would say : if I have known her,
You will say, she did embrace me as a husband,
And so extenuate the 'forehand sin :
No, Leonato,
                    I never tempted her with word too large ;
But, as a brother to his sister, show'd
Bashful sincerity and comely love.

Hero. And seem'd I ever otherwise to you ?

Claud. Out on thy seeming ! I will write against it
You seem to me as Dian in her orb,
As chaste as is the bud ere it be blown ;
But you are more intemperate in your blood
Than Venus, or those pamper'd animals
That rage in savage sensuality.

Hero. Is my lord well, that he doth speak so wide ?

Leon. Sweet prince, why speak not you?

D. Pedro.   What should I speak?

I stand dishonour'd, that have gone about

To link my dear friend to a common stale.

Leon. Are these things spoken? or do I but dream?

D. John. Sir, they are spoken, and these things are true.

Bene. This looks not like a nuptial.

Hero.   True!—O God!

Claud. Leonato, stand I here?

                    Is this the prince? Is this the prince's brother?

Is this face Hero's? Are our eyes our own?

Leon. All this is so; but what of this, my lord?

Claud. Let me but move one question to your daughter;

And, by that fatherly and kindly power

That you have in her, bid her answer truly.

Leon. I charge thee do so, as thou art my child.

Hero. O God, defend me! how am I beset!—

What kind of catechizing call you this?

Claud. To make you answer truly to your name.

Hero. Is it not Hero? Who can blot that name

With any just reproach?

Claud.   Marry, that can Hero:

Hero itself can blot out Hero's virtue.

What man was he talk'd with you yesternight

Out at your window, betwixt twelve and one?

Now, if you are a maid, answer to this.

Hero. I talk'd with no man at that hour, my lord.

D. Pedro. Why, then are you no maiden.—Leonato,

I am sorry you must hear: upon mine honour,

Myself, my brother, and this grievèd Count,

Did see her, hear her, at that hour last night,

Talk with a ruffian at her chamber-window;

Who hath, indeed, most like a liberal villain,

Confess'd the vile encounters they have had,

                    A thousand times in secret.

D. John. Fie, fie! they are not to be nam'd, my lord;

                              Not to be spoken of;

There is not chastity enough in language,

Without offence, to utter them. Thus, pretty lady,

I am sorry for thy much misgovernment.

   Claud. O Hero! what a Hero hadst thou been,

If half thy outward graces had been placed

About thy thoughts, and counsels of thy heart!

But, fare thee well, most foul, most fair! farewell,

Thou pure impiety, and impious purity!

For thee I'll lock up all the gates of love,

And on my eyelids shall conjecture hang,

To turn all beauty into thoughts of harm,

And never shall it more be gracious.

   Leon. Hath no man's dagger here a point for me?

                                   [Hero *swoons.*

   Beat. Why, how now, cousin! wherefore sink you down?

   D. John. Come, let us go. These things, come thus to light,

Smother her spirits up.

             [*Exeunt* Don Pedro, Don John, *and* Claudio.

   Bene.   How doth the lady?

   Beat.   Dead, I think!—help, uncle!—

Hero! why, Hero!—Uncle!—Signior Benedick!—friar!

   Leon. O fate, take not away thy heavy hand!

Death is the fairest cover for her shame,

That may be wish'd for.

   Beat.   How now, cousin Hero!

   Friar. Have comfort, lady,

   Leon.   Dost thou look up?

   Friar.   Yea, wherefore should she not?

   Leon. Wherefore! Why, doth not every earthly thing

Cry shame upon her? Could she here deny

The story that is printed in her blood?—

Do not live, Hero; do not not ope thine eyes:

For did I think thou wouldst not quickly die,

Thought I thy spirits were stronger than thy shames,

Myself would, on the rearward of reproaches,
Strike at thy life.   Griev'd I, I had but one ?
Chid I for that at frugal nature's frame ?
O, one too much by thee ! Why had I one ?
Why ever wast thou lovely in my eyes ?
Why had I not with charitable hand,
Took up a beggar's issue at my gates,
Who smirchèd thus, and mired with infamy,
I might have said, "No part of it is mine ;
This shame derives itself from unknown loins ?"
But mine, and mine I lov'd, and mine I prais'd,
And mine that I was proud on ; mine so much
That I myself was to myself not mine,
Valuing of her ; why, she—O, she is fallen
Into a pit of ink, that the wide sea
Hath drops too few to wash her clean again,
And salt too little, which may season give
To her foul tainted flesh !
  Bene.   Sir, sir, be patient.
For my part, I am so attir'd in wonder,
I know not what to say.
  Beat.   O, on my soul, my cousin is belied !
  Bene. Lady, were you her bedfellow last night ?
  Beat. No, truly, not ; although, until last night,
I have this twelvemonth been her bedfellow.
  Leon. Confirm'd, confirm'd !   O, that is stronger made,
Which was before barr'd up with ribs of iron !
Would the two princes lie ? and Claudio lie,
Who lov'd her so, that, speaking of her foulness,
Wash'd it with tears ?   Hence from her ! let her die.
  Friar.   Hear me a little ;
For I have only been silent so long,
And given way unto this course of fortune,
By noting of the lady : I have mark'd
A thousand blushing apparitions start
Into her face ; a thousand innocent shames

In angel whiteness beat away those blushes;
And in her eyes there hath appear'd a fire,
To burn the errors that these princes hold
Against her maiden truth. Call me a fool;
Trust not my reading, nor my observation,
Which with experimental seal doth warrant
The tenor of my book; trust not my age,
My reverence, calling, nor divinity,
If this sweet lady lie not guiltless here
Under some biting error.

  Leon.   Friar, it cannot be.
Thou seest that all the grace that she hath left,
Is, that she will not add to her damnation
A sin of perjury: she not denies it.
Why seek'st thou, then, to cover with excuse
That which appears in proper nakedness?

  Friar. Lady, what man is he you are accus'd of?

  Hero. They know, that do accuse me; I know none.
If I know more of any man alive,
Than that which maiden modesty doth warrant,
Let all my sins lack mercy!—O, my father!
Prove you that any man with me convers'd
At hours unmeet, or that I yesternight
Maintain'd the change of words with any creature,
Refuse me, hate me, torture me to death.

  Friar. There is some strange misprision in the princes.

  Bene. Two of them have the very bent of honour;
And if their wisdom be misled in this,
The practice of it lives in John the bastard,
Whose spirits toil in frame of villainies.

  Leon. I know not.   If they speak but truth of her,
These hands shall tear her; if they wrong her honour,
The proudest of them shall well hear of it.
Time hath not yet so dried this blood of mine,
Nor age so eat up my invention,
Nor fortune made such havoc of my means,

Nor my bad life reft me so much of friends,
But they shall find, awak'd in such a cause,
Both strength of limb, and policy of mind,
Ability in means, and choice of friends,
To quit me of them thoroughly.

    Friar.   Pause a while,
And let my counsel sway you in this case.
Your daughter, here, the princes left for dead:
Let her awhile be secretly kept in,
And publish it that she is dead indeed;
Maintain a mourning ostentation;
And on your family's old monument
Hang mournful epitaphs, and do all rites
That appertain unto a burial.

    Leon. What shall become of this? What will this do?

    Friar. Marry, this, well carried, shall on her behalf
Change slander to remorse;—that is some good:
But not for that dream I on this strange course,
But on this travail look for greater birth.
She dying, as it must be so maintain'd,
Upon the instant that she was accus'd,
Shall be lamented, pitied, and excused,
Of every hearer: for it so falls out,
That what we have we prize not to the worth,
Whiles we enjoy it; but being lack'd and lost,
Why, then we rack the value, then we find
The virtue, that possession would not show us
Whiles it was ours.—So will it fare with Claudio:
When he shall hear she died upon his words,
The idea of her life shall sweetly creep
Into his study of imagination;
And every lovely organ of her life
Shall come apparell'd into more precious habit,
More moving, delicate, and full of life,
Into the eye and prospect of his soul,
Than when she liv'd indeed:—then shall he mourn,

(If ever love had interest in his liver)
And wish he had not so accusèd her ;
No, though he thought his accusation true.
Let this be so, and doubt not but success
Will fashion the event in better shape
Than I can lay it down in likelihood.
But if all aim but this be levell'd false,
The supposition of the lady's death
Will quench the wonder of her infamy ;
And, if it sort not well, you may conceal her
(As best befits her wounded reputation)
In some reclusive and religious life,
Out of all eyes, tongues, minds, and injuries.

   Bene. Signior Leonato, let the friar advise you :
And though you know my inwardness and love
Is very much unto the prince and Claudio,
Yet, by mine honour, I will deal in this
As secretly, and justly, as your soul
Should with your body.

   Leon.   Being that I flow in grief,
                  The smallest twine may lead me.

   Friar. 'Tis well consented ; presently away ;
For to strange sores strangely they strain the cure.—
Come, lady, die to live : this wedding day,
Perhaps, is but prolong'd ; have patience, and endure.

           [*Exeunt* FRIAR, HERO, *and* LEONATO.

   Bene. Lady Beatrice, have you wept all this while ?
   Beat. Yea, and I will weep a while longer.
   Bene.   I will not
Desire that.
   Beat.   You have no reason ; I do it freely.
   Bene. Surely, I do believe your fair cousin is wronged.
   Beat. Ah ! how much might the man deserve of me,
That would right her !
   Bene.   Is there any way to show such friendship ?

                                         F

Beat. A very even way, but no such friend.

Bene. May a man do it?

Beat.   It is a man's office, but not yours.

Bene. I do love nothing in the world so well
As you; is not that strange?

Beat.   As strange as a thing I know not:
It were as possible for me to say, I loved nothing
So well as you: but believe me not; and yet
I lie not; I confess nothing, nor I deny
Nothing.—I am sorry for my cousin.

Bene.   By my sword,
Beatrice, thou lovest me.

Beat.   Do not swear by it and eat it.

Bene. I will swear by it that thou love me; and I will
Make him eat it, that says, I love you not.

Beat. Will you not eat your word?

Bene.   With no sauce that
Can be devised to it: I protest I love thee.

Beat. Why, then, God forgive me!

Bene.   What offence, sweet Beatrice?

Beat. You have staid me in a happy hour; I was about
To protest I loved you.

Bene.   And do it with all thy heart.

Beat. I love thee with so much of my heart, that none
Is left to protest.

Bene.   Come, bid me do anything for thee.

Beat. Kill Claudio.

Bene.   Ha! not for the wide world.

Beat.   You kill
Me, to deny it; farewell.

Bene.   Tarry, sweet Beatrice.

Beat. I am gone, though I am here:—there is no love in
          you:—
Nay, I pray you, let me go.

Bene.   Beatrice,—

Beat.   In faith, I will go.

Bene.   We'll be friends first.

Beat.   You dare
Easier be friends with me than fight with mine enemy.

Bene. Is Claudio thine enemy?

Beat.   Is he not approved
In the height a villain, that hath slandered, scorned,
Dishonoured my kinswoman?—O, that I were a man!—
What! bear her in hand until they came to take hands;
And then with public accusation, uncovered slander,
Unmitigated rancour,—O God, that I were a man!
I would eat his heart in the market place.

Bene.   Hear me, Beatrice;—

Beat. Talk with a man out of a window!—a proper saying!

Bene.   Nay, but Beatrice;—

Beat.   Sweet Hero!—
She is wronged, she is slandered, she is undone.

Bene.   Beat—

Beat. Princes and counties! Surely a princely testimony,
A goodly Count, Count Confect; a sweet gallant,
Surely!—O that I were a man for his sake!
Or that I had any friend would be a man
For my sake!   But manhood is melted into courtesies,
Valour into compliment, and men are only
Turned into tongue, and trim ones too: he is now
As valiant as Hercules, that only tells
A lie and swears it,—I cannot be a man with
Wishing, therefore I will die a woman with grieving.

Bene. Tarry, good Beatrice; by this hand I love thee.

Beat. Use it for my love some other way than swearing
    by it.

Bene. Think you in your soul, the Count Claudio hath
    wronged Hero?

Beat. Yea, as sure as I have a thought or a soul.

Bene. Enough! I am engaged; I will challenge him.
I will kiss your hand, and so leave you.   By this hand,
Claudio shall render me a dear account.

As you hear of me, so think of me. Go, comfort your
     cousin;
I must say she is dead; and so farewell.

SCENE II.—*A Prison.*

Enter DOGBERRY, VERJUICE, *and* SEXTON, *in gowns; and
     the* WATCH *with* CONRADE *and* BORACHIO.

Dogb. Is our whole dissembly appeared?
Verj.   O, a stool and a cushion for the sexton!
Sexton. Which be the malefactors?
Dogb.   Marry, that am I and my partner.
Verj. Nay, that's certain; we have the exhibition to
     examine.
Sexton. But which are the offenders that are to be
     examined?
Let them come before master constable.
Dogb.   Yea, marry;
Let them come before me.—What is your name, friend?
Bora.   Borachio.
Dogb. Pray write down—Borachio.—Yours, sirrah?
Con. I am a gentleman, sir, and my name is Conrade.
Dogb. Write   down—master   gentleman   Conrade.—
     Masters,
Do you serve God?
Con. Bora.   Yes, sir, we hope.
Dogb.   Write down—that they
Hope they serve God—and write God first; for God
Defend but God should go before such villains!
            Masters, it is proved
Already that you are little better than false knaves;
And it will go near to be thought so shortly. How answer
You for yourselves?
Con.   Marry, sir, we say we are none.
Dogb.   A marvellous

Witty fellow, I assure you; but I will go about with him.—
Come you hither, sirrah; a word in your ear, sir; I say to
       you,
It is thought you are false knaves.

    Bora.   Sir, I say to you, we are none.

    Dogb. Well, stand aside.—'Fore God, they are both in a
       tale.
                Have you writ down—that they are none?

    Sexton. Master constable, you go not the way to
       examine;
You must call forth the watch that are their accusers.

    Dogb. Yea, marry, that's the eftest way:—Let the watch
       come forth.—
Masters, I charge you, in the prince's name, accuse these
       men.

    Seacoal. This man said, sir, that Don John, the prince's
       brother,
Was a villain.

    Dogb. Write down—Prince John a villain.—Why this is
Flat perjury, to call a prince's brother—villain.

    Bora.   Master constable,—

    Dogb.   Pray thee, fellow, peace; I do not like thy look,
I promise thee.

    Sexton.   What heard you him say else?

    Seacoal.   Marry, that he
Had received a thousand ducats of Don John,
For accusing the lady Hero wrongfully.

    Dogb. Flat burglary, as ever was committed.

    Verj.   Yea, by the mass, that it is.

    Sexton.   What else, fellow?

    Seacoal. And that Count Claudio did mean, upon his
       words,
To disgrace Hero before the whole assembly, and
Not marry her.

    Dogb.   O villain! thou wilt be condemned
Into everlasting redemption for this.

Sexton.   What else?

Seacoal.   This is all.

Sexton. And this is more, masters, than you can deny.

Prince John is this morning secretly stolen away;

Hero was in this manner accused, in this very manner refused,

And upon the grief of this suddenly died.—Master constable,

Let these men be bound, and brought to Leonato's;

I will go before, and show him their examination. [*Exit.*

Dogb. Come, let them be opinioned.

Verj.   Let them be in the——

Con.   Hands off! coxcomb!

Dogb. God's my life! where's the sexton? let him write down

—The princes officer, coxcomb.—Come, bind them.—Thou naughty varlet!

Con. Away! you are an ass, you are an ass.

Dogb.   Dost thou not suspect

My place? Dost thou not suspect my years? O, that he were here

To write me down—an ass!—but masters, remember

That I am an ass; though it be not written down, yet forget not

That I am an ass.—No, thou villain, thou art full of

Piety, as shall be proved upon thee by good witness.

I am a wise fellow; and which is more, an officer;

And which is more, a householder; and which is more,

As pretty a piece of flesh as any in Messina;

And one that knows the law, go to; and a rich fellow enough, go to;

And a fellow that hath had losses; and one that hath

Two gowns, and everything handsome about him.—

Bring him away. O that I had been writ down—an ass.

ACT V.

SCENE I.—*Before* LEONATO'S *House.*

Enter LEONATO *and* ANTONIO.

Antonio.

F you go on thus, you will kill yourself;
And 'tis not wisdom, thus to second grief
Against yourself.

Leon.   I pray thee, cease thy counsel,
Which falls into mine ears as profitless
As water in a sieve.   Give not me counsel;
Nor let no comforter delight mine ear,
But such a one whose wrongs do suit with mine.
Bring me a father, that so lov'd his child,
Whose joy of her is overwhelm'd like mine,
                     And bid him speak of patience;
Measure his woe the length and breadth of mine,
And let it answer every strain for strain;
As thus for thus, and such a grief for such,
In every lineament, branch, shape, and form:
If such a one will smile, and stroke his beard;
Cry—sorrow, wag! and hem, when he should groan,
Patch grief with proverbs, make misfortune drunk
With candle-wasters,—bring him yet to me,
And I of him will gather patience.
But there is no such man: for, brother, men
Can counsel, and speak comfort to that grief
Which they themselves not feel; but, tasting it,
Their counsel turns to passion, which before
Would give preceptial medicine to rage,
Fetter strong madness in a silken thread,
Charm ache with air, and agony with words.

No, no; 'tis all men's office to speak patience
To those that wring under the load of sorrow:
But no man's virtue, nor sufficiency,
To be so moral, when he shall endure
The like himself.   Therefore give me no counsel:
My griefs cry louder than advertisement.

   Ant. Therein do men from children nothing differ.

   Leon. I pray thee, peace! I will be flesh and blood;
For there was never yet philosopher,
That could endure the toothache patiently;
However they have writ the style of gods,
And made a pish at chance and sufferance.

   Ant. Yet bend not all the harm upon yourself;
Make those, that do offend you, suffer too.

   Leon. There thou speak'st reason: nay, I will do so.
My soul doth tell me, Hero is belied;
And that shall Claudio know; so shall the prince,
And all of them, that thus dishonour her.

Enter DON PEDRO and CLAUDIO.

   Ant. Here come the prince and Claudio hastily.

   D. Pedro. Good den, good den.

   Claud.   Good day to both of you.

   Leon. Hear you, my lords,—

   D. Pedro.   We have some haste, Leonato.

   Leon. Some haste, my lord;—well, fare you well, my
     lord:—
Are you so hasty now?—well, all is one.

   D. Pedro. Nay, do not quarrel with us, good old man.

   Ant. If he could right himself with quarrelling,
                Some of us would lie low.

   Claud. Who wrongs him?

   Leon.   Marry, thou dost wrong me; thou
Dissembler, thou;—
     Nay, never lay thy hand upon thy sword;
I fear thee not.

Claud.   Marry, beshrew my hand,
If it should give your age such cause of fear:
In faith my hand meant nothing to my sword.

Leon. Tush, tush, man, never fleer and jest at me:
I speak not like a dotard, nor a fool,
As, under privilege of age, to brag
What I have done being young, or what would do
Were I not old.   Know, Claudio, to thy head,
Thou hast so wrong'd my innocent child and me,
That I am forc'd to lay my reverence by;
And, with grey hairs, and bruise of many days,
Do challenge thee to trial of a man.
I say, thou hast belied mine innocent child;
Thy slander has gone through and through her heart,
And she lies buried with her ancestors,—
O! in a tomb where never scandal slept,
Save this of hers fram'd by thy villainy.

Claud. My villainy!

Leon.   Thine, Claudio; thine, I say.

D. Pedro. You say not right, old man.

Leon.   My lord, my lord,
I'll prove it on his body, if he dare;
Despite his nice fence, and his active practice,
His May of youth, and bloom of lustyhood.

Claud. Away!   I will not have to do with you.

Leon. Canst thou so daff me? Thou hast kill'd my child;
If thou kill'st me, boy, thou shalt kill a man.

Ant. He shall kill two of us, and men indeed:
But that's no matter; let him kill one first;—
Win me and wear me,—let him answer me,—
Come, follow me, boy! come, sir boy, come follow me:
Sir boy, I'll whip you from your foining fence;
Nay, as I am a gentlemen, I will.

Leon.   Brother,—

Ant. Content yourself: God knows, I lov'd my niece;
And she is dead, slander'd to death by villains;

That dare as well answer a man indeed,
As I dare take a serpent by the tongue.
Boys, apes, braggarts, jacks, milksops!—

Leon.   Brother Antony,—

Ant. Hold you content. What, man ! I know them, yea,
And what they weigh, even to the utmost scruple :
Scambling, outfacing, fashion-mong'ring boys,
That lie, and cog, and flout, deprave, and slander,
Go anticly, and show outward hideousness,
And speak off half-a-dozen dangerous words,
How they might hurt their enemies, if they durst;
And this is all.

Leon.   But, brother Antony,—

Ant.   Come, 'tis no matter ;
Do not you meddle : let me deal in this.

D. Pedro. Gentlemen both, we will not wake your
          patience.
My heart is sorry for your daughter's death ;
But, on my honour, she was charg'd with nothing
But what was true, and very full of proof.

Leon. My lord, my lord,—

D. Pedro.   I will not hear you.

Leon   No !

Come, brother, away :—I will be heard ;—

Ant.   And shall, or some of us will smart for it.

          [*Exeunt* LEONATO *and* ANTONIO.

Enter BENEDICK.

D. Pedro. See, see ; here comes the man we went to seek.

Claud.   Now, signior,
What news ?

Bene.   Good day, my lord.

D. Pedro.   Welcome, signior : you
Are almost come to part almost a fray.

Claud. We had like to have had our two noses snapped
        off
With two old men without teeth.

D. Pedro.   Leonato and
His brother.   What thinkest thou?   Had we fought,
I doubt we should have been too young for them.

Bene. In a false quarrel there is no true valour.
I came to seek you both.

Claud.   We have been up and down
To seek thee; for we are high-proof melancholy, and
Would fain have it beaten away: wilt thou use thy wit?

Bene. It is in my scabbard; shall I draw it?

D. Pedro.   Dost
Thou wear thy wit by thy side?

Claud.   Never did any so;
Though very many have been beside their wit.
I will bid thee draw, as we do the minstrels; draw
To pleasure us.

D. Pedro.   As I am an honest man,
He looks pale.—Art thou sick or angry?

Claud.   What!
Courage, man!   What though care killed a cat,
Thou hast mettle enough in thee to kill care.

Bene. Sir, I shall meet your wit in the career,
An you charge it against me.   I pray you, choose
Another subject.

Claud.   Nay, then give him another staff;
This last was broke cross.

D. Pedro.   By this light, he changes
More and more; I think he be angry indeed.

Claud. If he be, he knows how to turn his girdle.

Bene.   Shall I
Speak a good word in your ear?   [*Whispers him.*

Claud.   God bless me from a challenge!

Bene. You are a villain;—I jest not:—I will make it
        good

How you dare, with what you dare, and when you dare.—
Do me right, or I will protest your cowardice.
You have killed a sweet lady, and her death shall
Fall heavy on you.   Let me hear from you.

    Claud. Well, I will meet you, so I may have good cheer.

    D. Pedro. What, a feast? a feast?

    Claud.   I' faith, I thank him; he
Hath bid me to a calf's head and a capon,
The which if I do not carve most curiously, say
My knife's naught.—Shall I not find a woodcock too?

    Bene. Sir, your wit ambles well; it goes easily.

    D. Pedro.   I'll tell thee
How Beatrice praised thy wit the other day.
I said thou hadst a fine wit: "True," says she,
" A fine little one."   " No," said I, " a great wit;"
" Right," says she, " a great gross one,"   " Nay," said I,
" A good wit;" " Just," says she, " it hurts nobody."
"Nay," said I, " the gentleman is wise;" " Certain,"
        said she,
" A wise gentleman."   " Nay," said I, " he hath the
        tongues;"
" That I believe," said she, " for he swore a thing to me on
Monday night which he forswore on Tuesday morning;
There's a double tongue; there's two tongues." Thus did
        she,
An hour together, trans-shape thy particular virtues;
Yet at last, she concluded with a sigh, thou wast
The properest man in Italy.

    Claud.   For the which
She wept heartily, and said she cared not.

    D. Pedro.   Yea,
That she did; but yet, for all that, an if
She did not hate him deadly she would love him
Dearly:—the old man's daughter told us all.

    Claud. All, all; and moreover, God saw him when he
                    Was hid in the garden.

D. Pedro. But when shall we set the savage bull's horns on
The sensible Benedick's head?

Claud.   Yea, and the text
Underneath, "Here dwells Benedick, the married man."

Bene. Fare you well, boy! you know my mind. I will
  leave
You now to your gossip-like humour; you break jests
As braggarts do their blades, which, God be thanked, hurt
  not.——
My lord, for your many courtesies I thank you:
I must discontinue your company: your brother, the
  bastard,
Is fled from Messina: you have among you killed
A sweet and innocent lady: for my lord Lackbeard there,
He and I shall meet; and till then, peace be with him.

                              [*Exit* BENEDICK.

D. Pedro. He is in earnest.

Claud.   In most profound earnest; and
I'll warrant you for the love of Beatrice.

D. Pedro. And hath challenged thee.

Claud.   Most sincerely.

D. Pedro.   What a pretty thing
Man is, when he goes in his doublet and hose,
And leaves off his wit.

Claud.   He is then a giant to an ape:
But then is an ape a doctor to such a man.

D. Pedro.   But, soft you, let me be;
Pluck up my heart and be sad! Did he not say
My brother was fled?

Enter DOGBERRY, VERJUICE, *and the* WATCH, *with*

CONRADE *and* BORACHIO *bound.*

Dogb.   Come you, sir; if justice cannot tame you,
She shall ne'er weigh more reasons in her balance.

Nay, an you be a cursing hypocrite,

               Once,—you must be looked to.

   D. Pedro. How now, two of my brother's men bound !

      Borachio

One.

   Claud. Hearken after their offence, my lord !

   D. Pedro. Officers, what offence have these men done ?

   Dogb. Marry, sir, they have committed false report ;

Moreover, they have spoken untruths ;

Secondarily, they are slanders ;

Sixth and lastly, they have belied a lady ;

Thirdly, they have verified unjust things ;

And, to conclude, they are lying knaves.

   D. Pedro. First, I ask thee what they have done ;

Thirdly, I ask thee what's their offence ;

Sixth and lastly, why they are committed ;

And to conclude, what you lay to their charge.

   Claud. Rightly reasoned, and in his own division ;

And, by my troth, there's one meaning well suited.

   D. Pedro. Whom have you offended, masters, that you

      are thus

Bound to your answer ? this learned constable

Is too cunning to be understood : what's your offence ?

   Bora. Sweet prince, let me go no further to mine answer :

Do you hear me, and let this Count kill me.

I have deceived even your very eyes :

What your wisdoms could not discover, these shallow fools

Have brought to light ; who in the night overheard me

Confessing to this man, how Don John, your brother,

Incensed me to slander the lady Hero ; how you

Were brought into the orchard, and saw me court Margaret

In Hero's garments ; how you disgraced her when you

Should marry her : my villainy they have upon record,

Which I had rather seal with my death, than repeat

Over to my shame : the lady is dead upon mine

And my master's false accusation ; and briefly

I desire nothing but the reward of a villain.

D. Pedro. Runs not this speech like iron through your
    blood?

Claud. I have drunk poison, whiles he uttered it.

D. Pedro. But did my brother set thee on to this?

Bora. Yea, and paid me richly for the practice of it.

D. Pedro. He is composed and framed of treachery:—
And fled he is upon this villainy.

Claud. Sweet Hero! now thy image doth appear
In the rare semblance that I loved it first.

Dogb. Come, bring away the plaintiffs; by this time
Our sexton hath reformed Signior Leonato of
The matter: and, masters, do not forget to specify,
When time and place shall serve, that I am an ass.

Verj. Here, here comes Signior Leonato, and
The sexton too.

    Re-enter LEONATO *and* ANTONIO, *with the* SEXTON.

Leon. Which is the villain? Let me see his eyes,
That, when I note another man like him,
I may avoid him. Which of these is he?

Bora. If you would know your wronger, look on me.

Leon. Art thou the slave, that with thy breath hast kill'd
Mine innocent child?

Bora.   Yea, even I alone.

Leon. No, not so, villain; thou beliest thyself;
Here stand a pair of honourable men,
A third is fled, that had a hand in it.—
I thank you, princes, for my daughter's death;
Record it with your high and worthy deeds;
'Twas bravely done, if you bethink you of it.

Claud. I know not how to pray your patience;
Yet I must speak. Choose your revenge yourself;
Impose me to what penance your invention
Can lay upon my sin: yet sinn'd I not,
But in mistaking.

D. Pedro.　　　　By my soul, nor I ;
And yet, to satisfy this good old man,
I would bend under any heavy weight
That he'll enjoin me to.

Leon.　　　　I cannot bid you bid my daughter live,
That were impossible ; but, I pray you both,
Possess the people in Messina here
How innocent she died : and, if your love
Can labour aught in sad invention,
Hang her an epitaph upon her tomb,
And sing it to her bones ;—sing it to-night.—
To-morrow morning come you to my house ;
And since you could not be my son-in-law,
Be yet my nephew : my brother hath a daughter,
Almost the copy of my child that's dead,
And she alone is heir to both of us ;
Give her the right you should have given her cousin,
And so dies my revenge.

Claud.　　　　　　O, noble sir !
Your over-kindness doth wring tears from me ?
I do embrace your offer ; and dispose
For henceforth of poor Claudio.

Leon.　　　To-morrow then I will expect your coming ;
To-night I take my leave.—This naughty man
Shall face to face be brought to Margaret,
Who, I believe, was pact in all this wrong,
Hir'd to it by your brother.

Bora. No, by my soul, she was not ;
Nor knew not what she did, when she spoke to me ;
But always hath been just and virtuous,
In anything that I do know by her.

Dog. Moreover, sir (which indeed is not under white
　　　and black),
This plaintiff here, the offender, did call me ass :
I beseech you, let it be remembered in his punishment.
And also the watch heard them talk of one Deformed

They say he wears a key in his ear, and a lock hanging
  by it;
      And borrows money in God's name,—
The which he hath used so long, and never paid,
That now men grow hard-hearted, and will lend nothing
For God's sake: pray you, examine him upon that point.

 Leon. I thank thee for thy care and honest pains.

 Dogb. Your worship speaks like a most thankful and
  reverend
Youth; and I praise God for you.

 Leon.   There's for thy pains.

 Dogb.   God save the foundation!

 Leon. Go, I discharge thee of thy prisoner, and I thank
  thee.

 Dogb. I leave an arrant knave with your worship; which
I beseech your worship to correct yourself, for the
Example of others. God keep your worship! I wish
Your worship well; God restore you to health! I humbly
Give you leave to depart; and if a merry meeting
May be wished, God prohibit it!—Come, neighbour.
    [*Exeunt* Dogberry, Verjuice, *and* Watch.

 Leon. Until to-morrow morning, lords, farewell.

 Ant. Farewell, my lords; we look for you to-morrow.

 D. Pedro. We will not fail.

 Claud.   To-night I'll mourn with Hero.
     [*Exeunt* Don Pedro *and* Claudio.

 Leon. Bring you these fellows on; we'll talk with
  Margaret,
How her acquaintance grew with this lewd fellow.
          [*Exeunt.*

SCENE II.—Leonato's *Garden.*

Enter Benedick *and* Margaret, *meeting.*

 Bene. Pray thee, sweet mistress Margaret, deserve well
  at
My hands, by helping me to the speech of Beatrice.

              G

Marg. Will you, then, write me a sonnet in praise of my
        beauty ?

Bene. In so high a style, Margaret, that no man living shall
Come over it; for in most comely truth, thou deservest it.

Marg. To have no man come over me ? why, shall I
        always
Keep them below stairs ?

Bene.   Thy wit is as quick as the greyhound's
Mouth,—it catches.

Mary.   And yours as blunt as the fencer's foils, which
Hit but hurt not.

Bene.   A most manly wit, Margaret; it will not
Hurt a woman: and so, I pray thee, call Beatrice:
I give thee the bucklers.

Mary.   Give us the swords; we have bucklers
Of our own.

Bene.   If you use them, Margaret, you must put in
The pikes with a vice; and they are dangerous weapons
For maids.

Mary.   Well, I will call Beatrice to you, who
I think hath legs.

Bene.   And therefore will come.

                                  [*Exit* MARGARET.

[Singing.]   *The god of love*
                    That sits above
                And knows me, and knows me,
                    How pitiful I deserve,—

I mean in singing; but in loving,
Leander the good swimmer, Troilus the first
Employer of panders, and a whole book-full
Of these quondam carpet-mongers, whose names yet
Run smoothly in the even road of a blank verse,—why,
They were never so truly turned over and over
As my poor self in love.   Marry, I cannot
Show it in rhyme: I have tried; I can find out
No rhyme to "lady" but "baby,"—an innocent rhyme;

For "scorn," " horn,"—a hard rhyme; for "school," "fool,"—
A baubling rhyme ; very ominous endings : no,
I was not born under a rhyming planet,
Nor I cannot woo in festival terms.—

Enter BEATRICE.

             Sweet Beatrice,
Wouldst thou come when I called thee ?
 Beat.   Yea, signior,
And depart when you bid me,
 Bene.   O, stay but till then !
 Beat.   " Then "
Is spoken; fare you well now :—and yet, ere I go,
Let me go with that I came for ; which is, with knowing
What hath passed between you and Claudio.
 Bene. Only foul words ; and thereupon I will kiss you.
 Beat. Foul words is but foul wind, and foul wind is
But foul breath, and foul breath is noisome; therefore
I will depart unkissed.
 Bene.   Thou hast frighted the word
Out of his right sense, so forcible is thy wit.
But I must tell thee plainly, Claudio
Undergoes my challenge ; and either I must shortly
Hear from him, or I will subscribe him a coward.
And, I pray thee now tell me, for which of my
Bad parts didst thou first fall in love with me ?
 Beat. For them all together ; which maintained so politic
    a state
Of evil, that they will not admit any good part
To intermingle with them.   But for which of my good parts
Did you first suffer love for me ?
 Bene.   Suffer love,—a good epithet !
I do suffer love indeed, for I love thee against my will.
 Beat. In spite of your heart, I think ; alas ! poor heart !
If you spite it for my sake, I will spite it for yours ;
For I will never love that which my friend hates.

               G 2

Bene. Thou and I are too wise to love peaceably.

Beat. It appears not by this confession; there's not
          one wise man

Among twenty, that will praise himself.

Bene.   An old,

An old instance, Beatrice, that lived in the time

Of the good neighbours: if a man do not erect in this age

His own tomb ere he dies, he shall live no longer

In monument than the bell rings and the widow weeps.

Beat. And how long is that, think you?

Bene.   Question!—

Why an hour in clamour, and a quarter in rheum:

Therefore it is most expedient for the wise (if Don Worm,

His conscience, find no impediment to the contrary)

To be the trumpet of his own virtues, as I am

To myself. So much for praising myself, who, I myself

Will bear witness, is praiseworthy. And now tell me,

How doth your cousin?

Beat.   Very ill.

Bene.   And how do you?

Beat. Very ill too.

Bene.   Serve God, love me, and mend.

There will I leave you too,

For here comes one in haste.

Enter URSULA.

Urs. Madam, you must come to your uncle. Yonder's old

Coil at home: it is proved my lady Hero

Hath been falsely accused; the prince and Claudio

Mightily abused; and Don John is the author of all,

Who is fled and gone. Will you come presently?

Beat. Will you go hear this news, signior?

Bene.   I will live

In thy heart, die in thy lap, and be buried in thy eyes;

And moreover, I will go with thee to thy uncle's.

                                        [*Exeunt.*

SCENE III.—*The Inside of a Church.*

Enter DON PEDRO, CLAUDIO, *and* ATTENDANTS, *with*
Music and Tapers.

Claud. Is this the monument of Leonato?

Atten.   It is, my lord,

Claud. [*Reads from a scroll.*]

> *Done to death by slanderous tongues*
>   *Was the Hero that here lies:*
> *Death, in guerdon of her wrongs,*
>   *Gives her fame which never dies.*
> *So the life, that died with shame,*
> *Lives in death with glorious fame.*
> *Hang thou there upon the tomb,*
>   [*Affixing the scroll.*
> *Praising her when I am dumb.*—

Now, music, sound, and sing your solemn hymn.

SONG.

> *Pardon, Goddess of the night,*
> *Those that slew thy virgin knight!*
> *For the which, with songs of woe,*
> *Round about her tomb they go.*
>   *Midnight, assist our moan!*
>   *Help us to sigh and groan,*
>   *Heavily, heavily!*
>   *Till death be uttered,*
>   *Graves yawn, and yield your dead,*
>   *Heavenly, heavenly.*

Claud. Now, unto thy bones good-night!—
    Yearly, will I do this rite.

D. Pedro. Good-morrow, masters; put your torches out:
The wolves have prey'd; and look, the gentle day,
Before the wheels of Phœbus, round about
Dapples the drowsy east with spots of grey.
Thanks to you all, and leave us; fare you well.

Claud. Good-morrow, masters; each his several way.

D. Pedro. Come, let us hence, and put on other weeds;
And then to Leonato's we will go.

Claud. And, Hymen, now with luckier issue speeds,
Than this, for whom we render'd up this woe!

[*Exeunt.*

SCENE IV.—*A Room in* LEONATO'S *House.*

Enter LEONATO, ANTONIO, BENEDICK, BEATRICE, MARGARET,
          URSULA, FRIAR, *and* HERO.

Friar. Did I not tell you she was innocent?

Leon. So are the prince and Claudio, who accus'd her
Upon the error that you heard debated:
But Margaret was in some fault for this,
Although against her will, as it appears
In the true course of all the question.

Ant. Well, I am glad that all things sort so well.

Bene. And so am I, being else by faith enforc'd
To call young Claudio to a reckoning for it.

Leon. Well, daughter, and you gentlewomen all,
Withdraw into a chamber by yourselves,
And, when I send for you, come hither masked:
The prince and Claudio promis'd by this hour
To visit me.—You know your office, brother;
You must be father to your brother's daughter,
And give her to young Claudio.   [*Exeunt ladies.*

Ant.   Which I will do with confirm'd countenance.

Bene. Friar, I must entreat your pains, I think.

Friar. To do what, signior?

Bene.   To bind me, or undo me, one of them.—
Signior Leonato, truth it is, good signior,
Your niece regards me with an eye of favour.

Leon. That eye my daughter lent her: 'tis most true.

Bene. And I do with an eye of love requite her.

Leon. The sight whereof, I think, you had from me,
From Claudio, and the prince: but what's your will?

Bene. Your answer, sir, is enigmatical :
But, for my will, my will is, your good will
May stand with ours, this day to be conjoin'd
In the estate of honourable marriage ;—
In which, good friar, I shall desire your help.
  Leon. My heart is with your liking.
  Friar.   And my help.
Here come the prince and Claudio.

   Enter Don Pedro *and* Claudio, *with Attendants.*

  D. Pedro. Good-morrow to this fair assembly.
  Leon. Good-morrow, prince ; good-morrow, Claudio.
We here attend you.   Are you yet determin'd
To-day to marry with my brother's daughter ?
  Claud. I'll hold my mind, were she an Ethiop.
  Leon. Call her forth, brother, here's the friar ready.
                             [*Exit* Antonio.
  D. Pedro. Good-morrow, Benedick.   Why what's the
     matter,
That you have such a February face,
So full of frost, of storm, and cloudiness ?
  Claud. I think, he thinks upon the savage bull :—
Tush, fear not, man ; we'll tip thy horns with gold,
And all Europa shall rejoice at thee ;
As once Europa did at lusty Jove,
When he would play the noble beast in love.
  Bene. Bull Jove, sir, had an amiable low :
And some such strange bull leap'd your father's cow,
And got a calf in that same noble feat,
Much like to you, for you have just his bleat.

   Re-enter Antonio, *with the ladies masked.*

  Claud. For this I owe you : here come other reckonings.
Which is the lady I must seize upon ?
  Ant. This same is she, and I do give you her.
  Claud. Why, then she's mine :—Sweet, let me see your
     face.

Leon. No, that you shall not, till you take her hand
Before this friar, and swear to marry her.

Claud. Give me your hand before this holy friar;
I am your husband, if you like of me.

Hero. And when I lived, I was your other wife:

[*Unmasking.*

And when you loved, you were my other husband.

Claud. Another Hero!

Hero.   Nothing certainer:
One Hero died defil'd; but I do live,
And, surely as I live, I am a maid.

D. Pedro. The former Hero! Hero that is dead!

Leon. She died, my lord, but whiles her slander lived.

Friar. All this amazement can I qualify;
When, after that the holy rites are ended,
I'll tell you largely of fair Hero's death:
Meantime, let wonder seem familiar,
And to the chapel let us presently.

Bene. Soft and fair, friar.—Which is Beatrice?

Beat. [*Unmasking.*]   I answer to that name. What is
    your will?

Bene. Do not you love me?

Beat.   Why, no; no more than reason.

Bene. Why, then your uncle and the prince and Claudio,
Have been deceived; they swore you did.

Beat.   Do not you love me?

Bene.   Troth, no; no more than reason.

Beat. Why, then, my cousin, Margaret, and Ursula,
Are much deceived; for they did swear you did.

Bene. They swore that you were almost sick for me.

Beat. They swore that you were well-nigh dead for me.

Bene. 'Tis no such matter.—Then you do not love me?

Beat. No truly, but in friendly recompense.

Leon. Come, cousin, I am sure you love the gentleman.

Claud. And I'll be sworn upon 't that he loves her;
For here's a paper written in his hand,

A halting sonnet of his own pure brain,
Fashion'd to Beatrice.

Hero.   And here's another
Writ in my cousin's hand, stol'n from her pocket,
Containing her affection unto Benedick.

Bene. A miracle! here's our own hands against our
        hearts!
Come, I will have thee; but, by this light, I take thee
For pity.

Beat.   I would not deny you;—but,
By this good day, I yield upon great persuasion;
And, partly, to save your life, for I was told
You were in a consumption.

Bene.   Peace! I will stop your mouth.
                              [*Kissing her.*

D. Pedro. How dost thou, Benedick, the married man?

Bene. I'll tell thee what, prince; a college of wit-crackers
Cannot flout me out of my humour. Dost thou
Think I care for a satire or an epigram? No;
If a man will be beaten with brains, 'a shall wear nothing
Handsome about him. In brief, since I do purpose to
Marry, I will think nothing to any purpose that
The world can say against it; and therefore never
Flout at me for what I have said against it; for
Man is a giddy thing, and this is my conclusion.—
For thy part, Claudio, I did think to have beaten thee;
But in that thou art like to be my kinsman,
Live unbruised, and love my cousin.

Claud.   I had well hoped
Thou wouldst have denied Beatrice, that I might
Have cudgelled thee out of thy single life, to make thee
A double dealer; which, out of question, thou wilt be, if
My cousin do not look exceeding narrowly to thee.

Bene. Come, come, we are friends. Let's have a dance
        ere we
Are married, that we may lighten our own hearts,

And our wives' heels.

   Leon.   We'll have dancing afterward.

   Bene. First, o' my word; therefore play, music.—Prince,
      thou art
Sad; get thee a wife, get thee a wife: there is no
Staff more reverend than one tipped with horn.

Enter a MESSENGER.

   Mess. My lord, your brother John is ta'en in flight,
And brought with armèd men back to Messina.

   Bene. Think not on him till to-morrow; I'll devise thee
Brave punishments for him.—Strike up, pipers!

[*Dance.*   *Exeunt.*

NOTES.

THE single quarto edition of "Much Ado about Nothing" was entered in the Stationers' Register in August, 1600 ; the play is not included in the enumeration of the poet's works by Meres in 1598, and we are thus led to the very probable inference that it was first produced in the intermediate twelvemonth—in Shakespeare's 35th year.

This quarto is the primary authority for the text ; the printers of the folio of 1623 are convicted of having used it, and carelessly enough, by their reproduction of its press errors—some score—they added at least thirty more of their own.   In moderate compensation, they plausibly inserted two monosyllables in a line of Beatrice (IV, 1)—

"Do not swear *by it*, and eat it,"

substituted, as plausibly, "heavenly, heavenly," for "heavily, heavily," as the last line of the dirge (V, 3) ; and, guided by rhyme, restored the word *dumb* a few lines above, in place of the usurping and impossible *dead*.

The not unsatisfactory division of Acts appears first in the folio.

The variations from the text of the quarto for which I have assumed responsibility are the following :—

For the impossible reading (II, 1)—

"It is the base though bitter disposition of Beatrice"—

I substitute, "It is nought but the," &c.   An accidental transposition —"It is the but nought"—would very easily induce a clumsy attempt at correction, producing the nonsense which we have to mend as we can.

I transpose the lines of the dirge—

"Till death be uttered

Graves yawn and yield their dead,"—

as an improvement at least on the unintelligible ;—but I withhold from substituting "*your* dead," for "*their* dead."

It is also with some effort that I abstain from printing Don Pedro's protest against a wordy preamble (I, 1)—

"Thou wilt be like a *lawyer* presently,

And tire the hearer with a book of words."

In reading *cause* for *kind* (IV, 1), I adopt a suggestion which Collier only made to renounce in making it.

In other cases my judgment as to corrections or corruptions by previous editors will be sufficiently indicated to the critics of text by the readings which, after full consideration always, I do or do not adopt.

Lightning Source UK Ltd.
Milton Keynes UK
UKOW04n0706210916

283481UK00020B/367/P